Babylonian Insurgency

Awakening to the Truth of Hell's Agenda

Mark Keener

Promising Truth Publishing

This book is dedicated to my Lord and Savior, Jesus Christ, who is Lord of all.

and

To my martyred loved ones.

TABLE OF CONTENTS

INTRODUCTION

THE DISSEMINATION OF the information contained in this book has been a long time in coming. I have been waiting many years to convey this story and it is a story that must be told. Every detail is factual, based upon my own personal experiences. Nothing has been fictionalized or exaggerated in any way; I am telling it exactly as it happened. An accurate understanding of this subject matter is crucial to the direction of the United States of America, which I, perhaps as you, dearly love. Most people possess no awareness of these things. You may find many of these revelations shocking and difficult to grasp. Please understand it is not my intention to elicit such a response. I am not motivated by personal agenda nor do I seek to entertain my readers. My aim is to inform as many people as possible about a very real agenda in existence that purposefully intends to usurp control over any and all facets of America, the God-given freedoms its Constitution was designed to protect, and our very way of life. This is the same mindset that resulted in Satan's expulsion from Heaven (Isaiah 14:12-20; Ezekiel 28:6-19). Scheming and planning for many years now, the architects of this agenda will do whatever it takes to achieve their objectives. Anyone who stands against them positions themselves in a very dangerous place. Make no mistake loved ones, this is a life-or-death battle to the finish. So it has been for me because I have stood up to them. When I was a young man, they had taken me under their wings, but as time went by it turned out I had already learned way too much about their way of doing things.

It is completely understandable to me if you wrestle with or question the truthfulness of what I am sharing. I would likely do the same thing if I were on the outside looking in, listening to another make claims such as are contained within the pages of this book. I will state this once again: I have no personal agenda or selfish ambition in writing this book. Truth is truth whether we accept it or not. Choosing not to believe something that is true does not render it false except within our own reasoning. As somebody once said, "Truth sounds like hate to those that hate the truth."

This is information that must be publicized not only for the benefit of the American people, but also for those beyond our own borders and for future generations as well. For several years now, I have encountered numerous hinderances in anticipation of this book's release. There exists an adversary who has done and will continue to do everything he can to prevent me from releasing this knowledge. I believe there is a strong probability that within our own legal system there has been opportunity for my sworn testimony which would serve so as to pull the cover off, exposing certain things. This would prove quite detrimental to those embracing that adversarial agenda. Simply due to the fact I know way too much, particular individuals possess strong motive to prevent such testimony in a court of law at all costs.

Reading this book and becoming informed may help you and many others avoid potentially treacherous pitfalls. Lives may be saved and our country as we have known it may continue to endure. Most importantly, souls may be saved from the eternal torment of Hell which would otherwise be their fate. Consider this a warning if nothing else. My prayer is that the apprehension of this knowledge facilitates an awakening throughout our great nation. God has clearly granted us something quite special here, but America faces many perils today. This is in large part due to our spiritual vision or rather, lack thereof. The people of the United States need to awaken to the truth of Hell's agenda. Allow me to rephrase that: we *must* awaken to the truth of Hell's agenda. We are in desperate need of a spiritual awakening.

As you read through the chapters of this book you will find the events described are, for the most part, in chronological order. Where I have taken the liberty of skipping around a little for the sake of continuity, dates are provided to help place events in proper sequence. It is my sincere hope and prayer that you will be blessed by what I share.

CHAPTER 1

CALLED FROM MY MOTHER'S WOMB

Before I formed you in the womb I knew you,
before you were born I set you apart.....

Jeremiah 1:5

TRUST US, THEY beckoned over and over again. Well-dressed prominent people repeatedly entered and exited the bedroom where I was floating above, gazing down upon them. If I began to trust them and believe what they were saying, then I would sink from my lofty levitation above to a height within their reach. Then they took advantage of that opportunity and came at me with harmful intentions. I quickly realized I must not confide in them, but instead keep my focus on a peaceful illumination emanating from above so as to remain aloft in a place where they could not bring me any harm. If I listened to their stories and began to trust them, my safety became compromised; they were not to be confided in, not in the least. If I continued to remain out of reach, they would exit just outside the bedroom door where they engaged in secret conversations with one another, scheming and devising ways to deceive me. Then they would return again inside my bedroom with a big smile and attempt to gain my trust. As long as I kept my focus, I remained out of their reach and no harm could befall me. On the wall outside the room immediately behind them were two golden masks. One displayed an eerie smile while the other wore a frown. Several decades later I reflected upon the presence of those masks and eventually came to understand their significance: These were the comedy and tragedy masks represented in ancient Greek drama. Their presence was in direct correlation to my experience working in Hollywood.

These dreams occurred throughout the earliest years of my life, each time with vivid imagery. They are my earliest memory. For so long I wondered at the clarity of what I experienced. Like all other people, I have encountered various dreams throughout my lifetime. Some were difficult to remember. Some I could recall short segments of, others longer portions. Then there are those born out of that incredible creative capacity our human minds possess which always elicit an amusing response upon recollection. Undoubtedly, you have had some whoppers yourself. In some of my dreams I found myself struggling with various circumstances and in various ways. The ones I really like, however, are those where I am flying, especially when I am able to do it well and fast while providing some kind of heroic assistance to others in need. Some dreams I experienced have been quite vivid, yet no dream I ever had contained the lucidity of the ones I had when floating in that room and I always wondered why. Who were these people? What was their objective? Why me and why was everything so clear? These floating dreams, so prominent early on, were removed from my dream experiences for many years to come. That was, until God's timing manifested with infallible precision.

Throughout Scripture, God uses a variety of methods to communicate with humanity, doing so with whomever He chooses. We observe Him working through dreams to give direction, guidance and even warning. During Joseph's experience in Egypt, God communicated by giving dreams to several of the individuals present in the story. He even communicated in the same manner to the adamantly defiant Pharaoh. Joseph himself had a prophetic dream before he ended up in Egypt, a dream so vivid that the dream rather had him. We read about descriptive and applicable dreams in Daniel. Hundreds of years later the New Testament opens up with a deluge of dreams, visions, and angelic visitations, then concludes with the Apostle John's Revelation received on the isle of Patmos. Although the Bible does not systematically teach on the subject of dreams, it cites many specific and significant examples, thereby validating their existence and utilization by God as a means of communicating to His creation. The Lord did it throughout the Old Testament, the Apostolic Age, and He continues to do so even today because in fact, "Jesus Christ is the same yesterday and today and forever" (Hebrews 13:8). I do think, however, that we really need to be cautious when people share their dreams with us while attempting to ascribe them as some-thing God has communicated to them. If in fact God is reaching out to us in such a way, the truth will ultimately be revealed, therefore you certainly have every right to question what I am sharing with you. As circumstances play out and time passes, the truth will be shown for what it is. As I stated in the introduction, I am not attempting to entertain you by putting this in print; I am simply stating everything as it happened. However, there is a matter of much greater signifi-cance involved. God has placed an unmistakable call upon my life and this message must go out. All that being said, we are told in Acts 2:17, repeated from the Old Testament Minor Prophet Joel, "In the last days, God says, I will pour out my Spirit on all people. Your sons and daughters will prophesy, your young men will see visions, your old men will dream dreams." We are in the last days, dear friends, and unmistakably so. If anyone happens to question that, then view-ing a television news broadcast may provide all the convincing one needs to believe this is true.

Many years passed before the meaning of those floating dreams became evident to me. It was about 2005 when they returned, this time with an addendum: Some of the perpetrators lost anonymity as people entering and exiting my bedroom began to assume specific identities. Some were people I had been working around, while others were particular political figures. Some remained still unidentifiable, as if perhaps yet to be at another time. The recurrence arrived with that same clarity the dreams held so many years prior. These were not dreams I simply remembered clearly after awakening. Rather, I was being shown something. Another significant aspect had also been divulged to me: The point of focus above that helped me stay safely afloat. The point of my focus is Jesus Christ. I am to remain focused upon Him, fixing my eyes upon Him (Hebrews 12:2, Colossians 3:1-2). Taking my focus off of Jesus in even the slightest way, for even the briefest moment is to compromise the safety I have in Him. I think that is far truer for every child of God than most of us begin to realize.

As the years past I never forgot those dreams; I remained mindful of them all along. I had another dream that is among my earliest memories. This one occurred with greater frequency throughout my lifetime, although less significant. In them, I would see myself running – running joyfully over rolling hills and across green fields. Sometimes the grass would be tall, other times it was short. At times the ground was level. It was something I had never shared with anybody and I really did not consider it necessary to do so. That was, until somebody else shared the specifics of my own dream with me.

It was 1986, the year I turned 20 years of age. I had been seriously contemplating my direction in life, more so than ever before. Some kind of career choice needed to be made, one that would provide for me well into my future. The thought of who God is and what He may have to say regarding this subject weighed upon me as well. During that time I considered becoming involved at a church, but which one should I go to? Is it even a church or is it some other place of worship? I knew all along God is real. All my life I had talked to Him. As a child I even attempted to approach and see Him, although that proved unsuccessful, at least to the extent of my ability to perceive Him. Not knowing Him on a personal level, I knew He was there. I did not *know* Him, but He knew me. He was quite aware of where I was at that point in life and that I was ready to step into my position within the Body of Christ. I was ready to step into place He prepared for me and called me to from my mother's womb.

Along came a knock on the door one day. Opening that front door, I observed a thin fellow, perhaps five to 10 years older than myself, exhibiting a radiant countenance upon his face and sporting a contagious smile. When he began to speak, his national identity became readily evident. Robroy was from a land down under and had stopped by to inquire about my dad's old sportscar parked in our driveway. He had recently made the acquisition of one similar and simply wanted to ask a few questions about ours to gain some insight that might be helpful to him for his restoration project. I gladly answered his questions during our pleasant, yet brief conversation. Afterwards, the cheerful fellow departed along his way and I figured that was all I would ever see of him.

The sound of a large vehicle pulling up to a stop in front my home had me peering out the window to observe what was going on. "Christian Life Church" read the sign painted on the side of a two-toned brown bus. Its door promptly opened and the sole occupant, its driver, came bouncing out with the joyful leaping of a frolicking fawn. Beaming with joy, the Australian lad had returned bringing with him once again that contagious smile. It had been a matter of days, perhaps a few weeks since I first met Robroy and there he was once again with a few more questions about the old sportscar. At least, that is what we thought he was doing there at that time and place. Jesus Christ, just like He did with the Samaritan woman at Jacob's Well in the Gospel of John Chapter 4, orchestrates divine appointments to this very day. As it turned out, this pleasant man was the assistant pastor at Christian Life Church, the congregation wherein I stepped into my appointed place within the Body of Christ for the first time. I am still connected with that congregation to this very day. They say hindsight is 20/20. With that clarity of vision, I can clearly see God choreographed those events as they occurred many years ago. An accurate retrospective analysis reveals nothing short of that very truth. God knew I was ready and He had the right person in place – a man sensitive to the direction of His Holy Spirit.

The 1980's were the time when MTV entered the American culture, becoming an instant hit. There was music by a popular band from a "Land Down Under" often playing on that new television channel, sounding out complete with a "Vegemite sandwich." Robroy had traveled to the United States with the ministry, Youth with A Mission, just a couple of years prior to share the Gospel in Los Angeles during the 1984 Summer Olympics. In the process of events, he connected with Christian Life Church and became a member of the pastoral staff. Sitting on a shelf in his office was a jar of Vegemite, a uniquely Australian gastronomic peculiarity. There I was, at a time in my life when I was becoming serious about things and was beginning to search out the truth about God. We did not realize it at the time, at least I did not, but that was the very reason Robroy was given a divine appointment. God used him to lead me to the proper place within His eternal family, to a place where I would become connected for all my existence henceforth. Thank you, God, and thank you Robroy for being sensitive to His direction. You see, God knew I was ready. I could have ended up at just any church, maybe even the wrong one. Our Creator deeply longs for an intimate, loving relationship with us and He was not about to let me errantly wander my own way into the wrong assembly of religious adherents. It is no mistake that God arranged this entire series of events in bringing me to the place where He wanted me to be. God made a divine appointment, sending to me a man from Australia named Robroy. With all honesty I can say that never in my entire life have I encountered another human being with the sensitivity to God's Holy Spirit that man possesses.

Several months after meeting him, Robroy and I were holding a conversation one day. I recall feeling somewhat awkward as he was staring deep into my eyes in a prolonged pause, his face displaying an undecipherable grin. He was not looking into my eyes, but rather seemingly through my eyes and into my spirit man. Earlier in this chapter I described dreams I had of myself jubilantly romping through green fields, dreams which I had never shared with anyone. Robroy seemed to be utilizing some kind of x-ray vision. 'What? What?!' I said to him. His face held that same beaming countenance it had when we first met. It was almost as if time paused as I waited for him to say something. Then the words began to come forth, "I see you…… running……. in fields of green." Those were his exact words and they still have me dumbfounded to this day. Robroy caught a glimpse of those dreams God gave me. With profound clarity, these words demonstrated unambiguous specificity in their application, bringing to life in illuminating fashion the Word of God spoken through the Old Testament prophet Joel:

> "And afterward, I will pour out my Spirit on all people. Your sons and daughters will prophesy, your old men will dream dreams, your young men will see visions. Even on my servants, both men and women, I will pour out my Spirit in those days. I will show wonders in the heavens and on the earth……."

> Joel 2:28-30a

CHAPTER 2

THAT'S SHOWBIZ BABY!

See, I set before you today life and prosperity, death and destruction.
For I command you today to love the LORD your God, to walk in
obedience to him, and to keep his commands, decrees and laws;
then you will live and increase, and the LORD
your God will bless you in the land you
are entering to possess.

Deuteronomy 30:15-16

SOMETIME AROUND THE middle of 1986 along came another
knock at the door. It was a friend who wanted to see if I would
join him working on a unique one-day job. There was a movie being filmed at a nightclub in Hollywood and they needed as many
people as they could round up to be the crowd for a rock concert
scene. I had no prior experience working in that business, but the
prospect of putting a few extra dollars in my pocket lured me into
going along with him on the last-minute adventure. Working in the
motion picture industry had never been on my radar at all, but it
did not stop there. Soon thereafter, another job opportunity in the
industry fell out of the sky right into my lap.

Another guy I knew became a security guard working on movie

sets. He called me one day saying the company he worked for needed more guards and asked if I was interested. In October of 1986 I
became employed full-time as a security guard in the motion picture
industry with Setwatch Security. Right away I was working 70 to 80
something hours a week while simultaneously attending classes in
community college. Prevailing minimum wage was $3.35 an hour at
that time and the security company paid just a few cents above that.
An abundance of overtime managed to increase the paycheck some.
Putting in 80 hours could net just over $400 for a week, miniscule
compensation by today's standards. The job involved simply keeping
watch over equipment and related items during both filming and off-
hours. On any given day we could be in a prestigious neighborhood
filming at a mansion, then the very next day we might film in the most
downtrodden of communities anywhere throughout the Los Angeles
area. Conversing with other guards, we often talked about what it
might be like to get a job on a crew, an aspiration that seemed out of
reach. As I soon learned, to get a good job working in this business
you really had to know somebody. Nowhere else did the saying ring
so true: 'It's not *what* you know, but *who* you know.'

When I began working in the industry as a security guard, my
very first task was to guard a filming location at Zuma Beach over the
weekend. The set was a collage of nipa huts constructed for a television series called *The A-Team*. My assignment was to keep curious
beachcombers from wandering into the huts and upon the wooden
walkways connecting them. To me, the beach was a very desirable
place to work; I often ventured out to Zuma anyway. Although the pay
was hardly above minimum wage, I was being paid to hang out at the
beach which was just fine with me. After a week or two at the Zuma
Beach location, I went on to work for that same company on a pleth-
ora of other well-known Hollywood productions. Among the recog-
nizable titles were *Highway to Heaven, Knott's Landing, Remington
Steele,* and *Spaceballs,* just to name just a few. There were many other
television shows, commercials, feature films, movies made for television, music videos, and on and on. Altogether, my time with that

company encompassed approximately two years before I moved on to bigger and better things in the industry.

David was one of my fellow guards at Setwatch. It was clear to see this was not a job he was going to continue doing for any length of time. He was an intelligent guy who wanted to become a cameraman in the industry, an aspiration he eventually did manage to achieve. Along the way David befriended someone on a film crew who was well connected in the industry. Before long he was offered a job working on a soundstage, employed directly by the production company. The job was similar to the security work we had been doing before, but this also included cleaning up around the stage and offices in addition to a variety of other miscellaneous tasks. When additional help was needed, David was asked if he knew another person they could bring in and he graciously considered me. After two years of doing security, I was taking my first small step up in show business.

The production was a new HBO television show based on an early 1950s E.C. Comics comic book series, *Tales from the Crypt*, written into screenplay. Six pilot episodes were planned for the gruesome irony. Working on the stage, I eagerly attempted to impress with a strong work ethic. Being young and healthy, I was afforded an employment opportunity that is not commonplace. After working on-stage a few weeks, it was decided some of the filming would be shot on location. My direct superior was a man brand new to the job himself. He possessed no previous experience in the industry, but was connected with the right people. It was asked of him to assemble the required crew and equipment necessary to lead the transportation department. David and I were included among a small handful of other guys brought on to be drivers. My boss began searching through the yellow pages for trucks and equipment to fulfill the task. Little did we know at that time, but eventually came to learn, equipment specific to that industry is rented from certain established people and their businesses; connecting with them is typically not achieved by searching through the yellow pages. There again, it is kind of a matter of *who you know*. I was nonetheless being afforded another unique opportunity. I became a driver as we took the production company out on location, beginning with a destination in Downtown Los Angeles.

As a young man in his early 20s, it really felt like I was moving up in the world and I was eager to impress with the opportunity I was afforded. Whether the task was security, cleaning the stage, breaking down sets and hauling the debris away, or driving equipment, I always gave it my best effort. I was young and had always been athletic, so I was in very good condition physically. Possessing the typical overabundance of pride a young man does, it had been my conscious objective to in no way allow any person around me anywhere, at any time, to demonstrate that they were anywhere close to working as hard as I was. It was always my determination to be the hardest working guy on any crew. The people I worked for did in fact observe my work ethic, at times acknowledged it, and kept me employed with them in various jobs for many years to come.

By the time 1992 rolled around I added stage laborer, security foreman, stage management, driver and craft service to my résumé. Between 1993 and 1998 I was offered several shows, but declined all but two feature films as I had begun to focus on a career in healthcare instead. I moved away in 1992, then ended up relocating back to Los Angeles late in 1998 and initiated a business venture in January of 1999. At that time I also went to work as a tram tour driver at Universal Studios, the job that finally granted me that coveted union membership. All in all, I worked on a long list of prominent Hollywood productions. Any attempt to list the entirety of them here would render a needlessly long inventory. If I did present that list, I am concerned it would give you the reader the perception I am attempting to impress people, which is in no way my motive. It is my desire to be completely transparent in making clear the point that the message being communicated by the composing of this book is not about me. Adhering to this understanding throughout my life has been challenging for me, especially when enduring adversity. I will therefore make a diligent effort to keep the main thing the main thing in communicating this message. It is within the nature of a human being to cry foul when subjected to injustices and I have faced more than my fair share of them. By experience, I have learned to fix my eyes on Jesus (Hebrews 12:2). God has His plan, this one in particular involves me, but it is not all about me. There is God's way. Then there is our way, which far too often deviates from what His perfect will is for us (Romans 12:2). Then, there exists yet still Hollywood's ways – that's showbiz, baby! It would not take long for me to learn how things work in this town.

CHAPTER 3

HOW THINGS WORK IN THIS TOWN

Again, the devil took him to a very high mountain and
showed him all the kingdoms of the world and their splendor.
"All this I will give you," he said, "if you will
bow down and worship me."

Matthew 4:8-9

ACHIEVING WHAT WAS seemingly impossible, David and I had become actual crew members of a major Hollywood production. As
happy and willing recipients, the big break appeared to just fall out of
the sky right into our laps. At the security company we were merely
hired guards, but now we were receiving paychecks directly from the
production company. It was a non-union show, at least for the time
being. After several weeks of filming at the private soundstage, it was
time to go on location. My boss was also the stage manager, his very
first jobs in the industry. His sister had become involved with the unit
production manager, the person producers hire directly under them
to oversee all the departments on a production. As my boss became
the transportation coordinator, David and I became drivers, a job that

included an increase in pay above what we had been receiving while working on the stage. Off we went, transporting trucks and equipment to Downtown L.A. on our first location.

Hollywood is said to have been the birthplace of film. The motion picture industry in Los Angeles has a culture all its own – a subculture within American society. Experienced, talented, and skilled labor exists in abundance here. I have personally witnessed individuals who possess remarkable talents and abilities, both in front of as well as behind the camera. Make no mistake though, if you intend to produce movies and television shows in this town, utilization of union labor is required. Filming permits are also necessary and local municipalities have special offices set up simply for this purpose. If and when a non-union show is issued a film permit, it does not escape the attention of union leadership; they soon find out. So does the non-union production.

I had felt quite smug in my newfound position as a driver. Initially, everything appeared to be running smoothly. There had been some small talk about the potential for the studio driver's union to picket us at the Downtown location, but nothing significant developed right away. The entire cast and crew, however, were staggeringly unprepared for what was headed our way. We were filming on the sidewalk at an intersection when a bus rolled by packed full of people who were hanging out of the windows shouting at us. "Here they come," I heard someone say near where the camera was set up. Within minutes, a cacophonous mob of bellicose men and women approached chanting and blowing horns. The signs they carried read, *"Tales from The Crypt Productions unfair to Teamsters Union Local 399."* It was subsequently explained to me that the unique opportunity I had been afforded was a job that belonged strictly to union members, or so the union claimed. They did everything within their ability to disrupt our filming and ultimately prevailed. After requesting to see our film permit, they noted a clause to intermittently halt pedestrian traffic was nowhere indicated. It was later suggested a pay-off had been prearranged so that what is otherwise a customary inclusion was conveniently overlooked. Knowing exactly what to do, as soon as the cameras began to roll, so did the mob. At the moment the director called out, "Rolling," picket signs and obnoxious horns were placed directly in front of the camera. Lea Thompson playing in the lead role attempted to perform, but simply could not. She sat down on the curb, put her face in her hands, and began to cry. Pompously pretentious, the picketing Teamsters even endeavored to provide her some consolation. We were unable to continue. The day was over for the cast and the crew. The union picketers, extensive destruction left behind in their wake, boarded that bus and departed. Myself and the other drivers were instructed to carefully inspect all equipment prior to transporting everything back to the stage. At least a couple of sliced sidewalls on tires were discovered. Roofing nails were everywhere on the street surface around the equipment, many already imbedded into the intended targets. Toilets in the honeywagon were clogged. Witnesses described two of the women picketers entering the bathrooms with their hands full of paper towels and other items that could clog sewage tanks. A crew member had his Mercedes Benz parked nearby. The entire hardtop roof of his car was full of dents the exact same size and shape as the ends of the *"unfair"* sign sticks. Questioning what the meanings of fair and unfair really are, we picked up the pieces and headed back to the stage.

Very little had been communicated regarding what ultimately became of our disastrous encounter in Downtown. It was communicated to me, however, that whenever the production filmed on location, I would be hired on as a driver. I relished this new job and was looking forward to continue in the occupation as long as it was available to me. That availability was far shorter lived than I ever could have imagined. The following week we were on location in Pasadena when out of nowhere two men walked up and said that they were drivers reporting for work. Soon thereafter, a few more arrived. As things turned out, the producers had negotiated with the Teamsters; the show would henceforth employ only union drivers. I was not a union driver nor were any of the others and it remained that way.

My boss, however, entered the union as a transportation coordinator while the rest of us were offered nothing at all in terms of union membership. What I was offered right then and there that day in Pasadena was a steel tine garden rake and a push broom. My new job was to clear off a large concrete area covered a foot thick in ivy and leaves, then help the caterer set up for lunch. I had been demoted back to general laborer, but at least I still had a job.

The motion picture industry continues to be an integral constituent of the Los Angeles economy. Over the years its trade unions have become interwoven into the fabric of politics. For many years to come I would be employed in this business and it was good and profitable for me in a variety of ways. More importantly than considering how it benefitted me, however, is to accurately understand what God had been doing all along. He had not revealed it to me at the time, but I was going to be used by Him for His specific purposes. After all, I had been called to this from my mother's womb. As my dearly departed pastor Dr. Jones used to say, "Put your big boy britches on!" Donning that euphemistic pair of pants and a good pair of shoes, I treaded forward.

PUTTING MY SHOES ON

Taking him by the right hand, he helped him up,
and instantly the man's feet and ankles became strong.
He jumped to his feet and began to walk.

Acts 3:7-8a

I ONCE HEARD Aaron Spelling speak about his appreciation for a certain well-known Hollywood starlet. As one of the most prolific producers in the business, he was the one who provided her the opportunity that brought the notoriety, fame, and fortune she came to enjoy. Several years later, Mr. Spelling was producing another project which went on to become quite popular. He contacted that actress, asking her to join the cast of the new show and she willingly obliged. Spelling said that he put shoes on her and she never walked away as pretty much all others do. When a person works in this business, they are looking to get their shoes on. If they are an actor or actress, they pursue membership in the Screen Actors Guild and to become a star, so to say, and make it big. For crew members, the prevailing aim is to get in the union of their respective trade, whatever their craft may be. From that point on they receive a higher, locked-in wage, have superb benefits, and acquire incredible, even at times unreasonable, job protection. Once you have your shoes on, you really have no need of those who helped you get there in the first place. One may simply "walk away."

Tales from The Crypt experienced a fair amount of success, running for several seasons and putting out two feature films. The second season of the series found us on a new, yet still independent soundstage where I was kept on as stage/general laborer. Although the drivers became union, the remainder of the crew members were not. That included the craft service guy who did not show up on the first day of filming. Leading up to that first day, there was much to do to get everything in place and ready to go. There were several days of preparation involved. Various equipment had to be brought in, organized, and set up. For craft service, the supplies, beverages, and food products were purchased and readied for the cast and crew, all stocked up and ready to serve. My tasks had involved preparing the soundstage. Besides cleaning and maintaining the stage, fire lanes, required by law, needed to be measured out and clearly marked throughout the interior perimeter. Fire extinguishers and lighted emergency exit signs were installed. Red light and bell systems were constructed, as is standard on sound stages, so that people are quiet and not entering and exiting through doors while cameras are rolling. Designated work and storage areas for the various departments were constructed. On and on it went: fire sprinkler systems, sound baffling on the walls, various office arrangements, required permitting, and inspections all demanded time and preparation. Up to that point I had been working 12-hour shifts, seven days a week for several weeks leading up to the opening day of principal photography. In the last big push I worked three consecutive shifts for a total of 36 hours straight and boy, was I tired! That Monday morning I was quite ready to go home, shower, and sleep. The crew began to arrive, but where was the craft service guy? He was nowhere to be found and they were unsuccessful in their attempts to reach him. He had been there throughout the preceding week or two, getting everything ready and in place, but now appeared to be abandoning his job. As it turned out, he was enduring

a significant personal challenge which I was told he was eventually able to overcome. In the meantime, everything needed to provide craft services to the crew was in place except for the craft service guy himself. This fellow was actually the younger brother of my boss who ended up approaching me as I had been his go-to, righthand man. As exhausted as I was, I was not permitted to leave. At first, we thought it would simply be a matter of setting up and maintaining the craft service table until he arrived. Hour after hour passed into what evolved into something in the neighborhood of an 18-hour work day and he never did show up. After we learned what was going on with him, I was asked to return the next day. I unpreparedly inherited a position which I had absolutely no experience in. Forgoing any training even as an assistant to another and without any person to assist me, I figured out what to do and how to do it. Some kind of prior experience would certainly have been helpful. Even a helper would have made the job much easier. Craft service is not a job that requires the intellect of an extreme genius, therefore I was able to perform the necessary duties. I ended up doing that job for the next two or three seasons on *Tales*. After that I became the assistant stage manager for a season or two, the phantom position my boss's brother had received after defaulting on craft service. Unlike him in that position though, I was present, visible, and performed the duties of the job. As assistant stage manager I received a very slight pay raise, worked only 12-hour shifts, and had a much easier position. At that time I was okay with all that, but there were a number of things my conscience would ultimately come to find morally objectionable.

Of all the drivers working those six pilot episodes on *Tales from the Crypt*, it was only my boss who procured union membership. He got in as a result of the union/producer negotiations following the riot/strike in Downtown at our first location. With no previous experience, he instantly became the transportation coordinator, which is the head person of that department. He was simultaneously the stage manager on *Tales*, concurrently receiving paychecks for each position. It was clearly evident he was donning newfound footwear of his own. As for me, it seemed the shoes I was putting on were the same old worn-out sneakers I had been wearing all along. What was that saying I mentioned earlier? Oh yeah, 'It's not *what* you know, but *who* you know.'

During those days as craft service and assistant stage manager, some of the regular drivers on the show took me under their wings, including the Transportation Captain. The captain is a sort of foreman, the coordinator's righthand man. I went on to become close friends with both that captain and his co-captain. I was young, still in my early 20s, and they were like father figures to me. They told me if obtained a Class A Commercial Driver's License, then they would get me into the Teamsters Union, Hollywood Studio Drivers Local 399. How could I pass that up?! So that is exactly what I did and in short order. When I got the license so quickly it surprised them. They said that they had never seen anyone obtain a Class A License so fast. They described to me how they had seen others struggle with difficulty even on the written tests. I really did not find it so problematic. This was a unique opportunity that is not available to very many people. That is, unless you know somebody.

As my first few years in the industry passed by, I had come to make a few personal connections and I was learning the ropes – that is, how things work in Tinseltown. The gears were in the works for me to ditch the old sneakers and gain for myself more formidable footwear. On the other hand, God had been preparing me to receive His provision: feet fitted with the readiness that comes from the gospel of peace (Ephesians 6:15). Throughout the entire process I learned by direct observation and personal experience, not all that glitters is gold.

CHAPTER 5

NOT ALL THAT GLITTERS IS GOLD

"Here now is the man who did not make God his
stronghold but trusted in his great wealth
and grew strong by destroying others!"

Psalm 52:7

THE RAIN WAS coming down consistent that night and hard at times, but I was dry and comfortable sitting in the heated maxivan with the drivers. The crew was primarily interested in coffee and other hot beverages, so my craft service table was not requiring much of my attention. It was another 18-plus-hour workday for me, this one an all-nighter at Franklin Canyon Reservoir. This is a common filming location in the Santa Monica Mountains just off Coldwater Canyon near Mulholland Drive and has been used often for many years. You have undoubtedly seen it yourself on television and movie screens. The opening segment of the *Andy Griffith Show* was filmed there – the part where Sheriff Andy is walking with the young Ronnie Howard next to a small, treed lake with fishing poles on their shoulders. I had been there several times during my earlier security guard days and would be there again many more times throughout the ensuing years. Whenever *Tales* went on location, a few more drivers were brought on due to the additional vehicular equipment utilized in the process of the production. I always hung out with the drivers. Sometimes there would arise a certain task that needed to be performed, one that they would rather take a pass on, but which of course required a union driver nonetheless. Often it would be a matter of something needing to be picked up or dropped off across town and I would fill that void as their quasi-son in training. It was on that very night I received some of my first briefings on how "we do things." These infrequent conversations, rather indoctrinations, addressed the internal mechanisms of a movement, going well beyond the reputation and influence of their union. Outsiders are in no way privy to the insider knowledge which was being shared with me. The Transportation Captain had suggested to the other drivers that they should be careful just how much they told me because I was "not in yet." That night, however, a lot was said. This was information that, many years down the road, placed me in a position of knowing too much and as destiny proved, way too much. That was not the only time such privileged insider knowledge was shared with me. For a number of years I had somewhat idolized these guys and their union. They were powerful, earned a significant income, and had a cushy job. When it is cold and raining like that night at Franklin Canyon, the crew may be out in the elements, but drivers are cozy sitting in a van, dry and warm. When it is scorching hot, they are sitting in the van with the air conditioning on full blast sipping on a cold beverage. Working long hours, as such is the circumstance in this business, renders a person sleep deprived. The drivers control every piece of equipment that moves. If one of them feels overcome by human limitations and desires a little shut-eye, then they, unlike others on set can so easily do, cover for each other as one grabs some sleep on a bed or couch in a trailer. Collectively bargained union contracts require hot sit-down meals to be provided at no charge, available one hour prior to assigned call time and every six hours thereafter. If a meal is missed for some reason, then meal penalty compensation is added to one's paycheck. The benefits are extensive and quite good, unlike any of the many other places I have worked. It always struck me as uncanny when hearing occasional complaints coming from crew members about a caterer's food or about some other thing they were unhappy about. In all honesty, these routine meals are banquets fit for dignitaries. My opinion is that producers generally treat their employees quite well, especially when obligated via contractual agreement. As for the meal items served, if there is an item you do not like, then there is always a cornucopia of alternatives to choose from. What other job has any of us ever held that feeds us at all, let alone like kings and queens each and every workday as an indubitable requirement of a negotiated contract?

There were many things I thought were wonderful about working in the industry. One of my driver friends used to say, "Benefit of the business," with his simulated mafioso-like accent, referring to the many ways we made income or gained something otherwise. Drivers often own a truck which will be placed on rental on the show, providing them an additional source of income. Some own many pieces of equipment. It is a really nice perk, but the dishonesty and corruption that I have personally witnessed in association with it is something that is really quite troubling. Sometimes equipment that was on rental was being rented simultaneously onto other shows. Oftentimes the item did not even exist at all, but was "on rental." This was true not only for transportation equipment, but also for wherever such shenanigans could be pulled off otherwise. For example, people on payroll were not always present, extra hours were routinely added to timecards, and work would be performed at somebody's home while on production payroll. Services were paid for although not actually provided. Receipts were turned in for just about anything and everything. Superfluous strategies were profiting people in multiplicative manners. There I was, one of their boys, being brought up under their wings and learning the ropes.

Christians working in Hollywood are in no way a commonplace occurrence. I have personally met and known very few and they were somewhat adept at concealing their faith and for good reason. Most people employed in the entertainment industry possess strong liberal values and in my observation are simply intolerant of contrary, un-shared viewpoints. When I was a security guard early on, there was a crew member on a show who arrived at crew parking where I was assigned to watch crew cars. This guy was a Christian and vocal about his faith, a welcome sight to my eyes. He exhibited the countenance of a man who had just come out of a time of deep worship and was exceedingly joyful as he excitedly told every person within earshot about Jesus. It was clear he did not rub well upon some of the drivers as I heard some grumbling about him among them as they transport-ed crew members from crew parking to the set that morning. My as-signed position was to remain in that lot and watch over the safety of the crew's automobiles. Around lunchtime, as was the norm, a driver arrived in a van. Sometimes they would bring lunch to the guard or someone else would rotate over and cover so that guard could leave his post to go have a meal. On this occasion two maxivans pulled into the lot. One drove directly over to that Christian brother's car, block-ing its view. The other van driver came to me and told me to hop in so we could go get lunch, so I did. When we returned, two men were kneeling over doing something beside that fellow's car. Before I could see anything, they both got into that other van and drove away. At the conclusion of what was a typical long work day, the crew was being transported via maxivan back to crew parking. When that Christian brother got into his car, it would not start. These were the days before everyone was carrying a cellphone, so that guy was asking the drivers for help. It was really quite sinister, the way they mocked him, laugh-ing at times. They said things like, "Now how did that happen?" and "The devil must've done it!" I would go on to hear these same exact words a number of times during my showbiz experience. I was just 20 years old, young and uninformed at that particular time, and did not know what to say in response to the fellow's dilemma. I decided it was in my best interest to simply refrain from engaging the situa-tion. I kept my mouth shut and stayed out of it. The poor guy began to

suspect that perhaps they had something to do with it. He hesitantly asked, "You guys didn't" or "wouldn't" or something to that effect, his face absent the illuminating joy he exhibited earlier that day. That young man's vehicle ended up being pulled onto a flatbed tow truck and hauled away. I never saw him again.

When a production company goes on location, much space is required for a variety of needs. A lot may be rented as a place for a base camp, catering, crew parking, or even for the actual set itself. Sometimes equipment is positioned on public streets where permits are obtained and temporary no parking signs are posted a few days prior. Once, when I was a driver on a movie made for television, we were filming near MacArthur Park and needed parking for our trucks on what was a fairly busy street. For whatever reason, the location manager failed to acquire a permit for one certain stretch of a city block, but the on-set police officer came to the rescue. He happened to have with him several blank *Temporary No Parking* signs. With the help of a location manager, they simply wrote the dates and times on the signs, posted them, and even went so far as to have one or two of the cars that were parked there cited and towed away. At the time I actually considered the act not only acceptable, but quite helpful in achieving our purposes. Over time, however, such things really began to wear upon me.

When 1992 arrived I had been working in showbiz nearly six years and once again found myself on another season of *Tales from the Crypt*. Although sometimes a handful returned, most crew members changed with each successive season. As for me, the actual job I was hired to do would be different this time around: I was given the job of assistant to the head of security. Our stage was a converted warehouse on Balboa Boulevard in Van Nuys. Parking was limited, proving to be a challenge as the crew had been required to park their vehicles on the busy boulevard and across it in a residential area. Oftentimes, somebody would drive into the lot at the rear of the stage and attempt to park on premises, which was prohibited. If a drop-off of materials or equipment was needed, then it would be permitted as long as they promptly removed the vehicle afterward. As security for the production, it was among my assigned duties to monitor proper adherence to these rules.

One day a late model shiny Lincoln Town Car with two male occupants drove in past me, completely disregarding my attempts to stop them. They proceeded into the rear lot and pulled into a parking spot. When the two men exited the vehicle I immediately, yet politely informed them that they were not allowed to park in the lot. One of the men, exhibiting a pugnacious disposition, demanded to know not only who I actually was, but who I thought I was. Properly advising him of my identity and duties did not appease his angry approach. The other man, with a gentle wafting of his hand, told the irate fellow that he would handle the situation. "Do you have a radio?" he inquired of me. As security we carried two-way radios, communicating with one another and also with the front office. The man asked me to radio in to the office to announce their presence. Let them know "Leo T. Reed and Tony Cusumano" are here out back, him being Leo, his fuming sidekick Tony. Reflecting back upon it I find it quite comical as I had called in over the radio, repeating their names exactly as he had stated them to me, complete with the "T." in Leo T. Reed. There was an unusual period of radio silence as I awaited a response. Suddenly, the rear door of the building opened as F.A. Miller, the production manager, came hobbling out with his cane. F.A. thanked and excused me, saying he would handle it from there. Using a cane due to a disability affecting his lower extremities, F.A. had moved extraordinarily fast from the front office and through the stage where he emerged from that door. Leo, as it turned out, was the head guy of the Teamster's Local 399 Studio Driver's Union. Tony was his sidekick, his righthand man, a guy I would sit down to lunch with some eight or nine years later as I further detail in chapter eight. After Leo and Tony went on their way that day, F.A. expressed his gratitude, stating he was very appreciative of me intercepting them and not allowing them to wander onto the stage and into the offices. F.A. divulged a little more than a hint regarding what they had come for. There was a complaint received in the 399 Local office regarding the way affairs were being conducted in the transportation department. For quite some time I had already been aware of certain underhanded financial dealings. F.A. was quite fond of that transportation coordinator and would cover for him in any way necessary. He told me a sizable payoff was required to placate the probing union heads while business as usual continued in the transportation department unchanged. I eventually learned from F.A. himself that he and these men did not exactly harbor strong heart-felt sympathies for each other.

During that same season on *Tales*, circumstances proved that we had a few members of our crew who were ready and willing to perform Satan's dastardly deeds. I had already heard several years prior about certain poisons used on people who got in the way and/or became designated targets. That Spring on *Tales* some of them decided to take advantage of the occasion and have a little fun. The man who was the transportation captain this time around and an assistant stage manager, who was a driver in the making, were the primary perpetrators. To them this was nothing more than playtime. They did not intend any real harm; it was a matter of entertainment. The agent employed was Ipecac, an over-the-counter medication used to induce vomiting which I had never heard of prior to that. These two guys, along with a couple of others, targeted certain people on the crew they did not like by adulterating something they consumed with Ipecac, causing them to throw up. When I voiced opposition to their dastardly deeds, I found myself ostracized from their clandestine insider group. That transportation captain, a highly questionable character at best, began exhibiting a distinct disdain for me. I was a right-hand man for his boss whom he despised due to their soured business dealings. I suspect he was the one who dropped the dime summoning Leo and Tony to our stage.

Later during that same season on *Tales*, one of the guys was heading over to pick up burgers and fries at a popular eatery nearby. The thought of what these guys had been doing did come to my mind at the time, but I really did not think they would target me. After all, "The devil must've done it!" Right? When I was asked if I wanted anything,

I ordered chili fries. When the food arrived back in the office, I was not able to get to it right away. When I finally did, that assistant stage manager was alone there in the office where my chili fries were. I was a bit apprehensive, but stupid me, I ate it anyway. By the time I finished my tummy was feeling a bit unsettled. I walked out of the office, the uneasiness of my stomach rapidly increasing. Within seconds I was bolting for the restroom. Never before or ever since have I experienced such forceful, violent vomiting. It was unmistakably clear I had fallen victim to what they held within their own reasoning to be comical entertainment. It seemed to me an appropriate cause-and-effect service of justice that very little of my emesis actually found its way into any commode. A vast portion of the bathroom floor was indeed a mess. For some strange reason, sinks and toilets were as well by the time I finished. Mulling over the situation and realizing precisely what had occurred, I exited the restroom before anyone was able to witness the party who created the catastrophic disaster. Leaving it completely intact where it was, the stage managers, willing participants in the nefarious endeavor, eventually discovered the disastrous muddle which was their responsibility to rectify. Undoubtedly, they knew the source, but nothing was ever said about it to me. Oddly enough, that appeared to be the end of their Ipecac laced misdeeds as I do not recall hearing any more about it for the remainder of that season.

Not too long after that '92 season on *Tales*, however, I did hear of something I found quite disturbing, especially in light of my knowledge regarding how these guys operate. That same assistant stage manager had become married along the way. After a while, I heard he began experiencing difficulties in his relationship with his wife and the word divorce came up in conversation. I recall meeting her only once or twice myself and honestly, I wondered what a nice girl like her was doing with that dude. The marriage was not very old and neither was she. The circumstances conveyed within weeks or months thereafter were such that his wife had been unexpectedly diagnosed with an aggressive form of cancer which took her life in a relatively brief amount of time. In my own thinking that certainly brought up a few questions, answers to which I can only provide with some measure of conjecture. You may draw your own conclusions and perhaps that was nothing more than a terribly unfortunate tragedy. Yet, considering the players involved and the manner in which whey execute business, business may not have been all that was executed.

So, what do they do when it goes beyond simple playful entertainment, when it involves somebody who really stands against them? What if you upset them or actually posed a real threat to them in some way? Remember that strike/riot in Downtown Los Angeles a few years prior? How about that Christian brother sharing about the love of Jesus whose vehicle suddenly became inoperable? What would happen to an unsuspecting person who ended up in the crosshairs of their sights for more serious reasons? Maybe you can begin to imagine the possibilities. Believe me dear ones, this is by no means any place you ever want to end up in.

Laid upon my tympanic membranes during the first five months of 1992 came a few more insightful divulgences regarding the reprehensible clandestine exploits performed by a certain segment of individuals. Perhaps one can apply to this gang a no more suitable label than, workers of iniquity. These revelations further served to reinforce my decision to move on to a different career. One specific story impacted me in such a way as to bring a little more understanding to the reality of what I had discovered regarding who these people are and what they are capable of.

During that last season of *Tales*, another driver recounted his own personal experience, describing how he himself had been taken into custody by the L.A.P.D., arrested for drunk driving. He had admittedly consumed alcohol. When and where he described, but those details were not retained in the memory bank of my human brain. What I do recall him saying though, is something nobody could ever forget. He told of how he was taken to a police station in the San Fernando Valley. The man went on to laughingly tell that when he gained access to the phone call he was entitled to, he did not call a lawyer, a bail bondsman, nor his wife. He called, of all people, the union office. According to him, it took a fairly short amount of time to receive the relief he sought. He explained that Leo, the union head, arrived at the police station and subsequently secured his release. Laughingly perhaps is an understatement. It was really more mockingly, as if he carried a predisposition of some kind of immunity as an insider member of that union. That man described the story of how he was released from custody sans citation or court date. He said that none were given and that was the end of the story. No appearances, no fines, and no criminal charges. That was simply the end of it!

I suppose just a couple of years or more prior, his story would have been something I found respectable and dignified. It may have even given me a stronger desire to be a part of this perceivably elite group; all the more I would have wanted to be one of them. That was not to be as the presence of Jesus Christ in me over the previous six years became evidenced by His transforming work. My values were no longer predicated upon selfish ambition and worldly gain. As a result, Hollywood's ways were something I had increasingly found repulsive. The glamour of showbiz was fading fast as the realization fell upon me: Not all that glitters is gold.

When I heard such stories from these guys, the information was at first difficult to digest. Then as time when on and I learned more, the reality of what they had been sharing was settling in. Along the way, some the events they described I had become eyewitness to myself. That was absolutely nothing compared to how they would prove themselves in time to come. Isn't fiction limited to something portrayed on television and movie screens? Could it really be that the extreme radical agenda this group possessed was far truer than I had previously considered it to be? The motion picture industry was beneficial to me in some ways, but I eventually realized that on second thought, I don't wanna work here anymore.

CHAPTER 6

ON SECOND THOUGHT, I DON'T WANNA WORK HERE

What good is it for someone to gain the whole world,
yet forfeit their soul? Or what can
anyone give in exchange for their soul?

Mark 8:36-37

AFTER ABOUT SIX years of working in the motion picture industry, I was seriously reconsidering the prospect of continuing my employment there. I had grown in my faith during that time and heavy conviction was coming upon me. In a way it seemed as if the Lord did want me there, but the dark ways of that business began to substantially diminish the lure of Tinseltown. The bright lights of Hollywood were fading fast.

Corruption and embezzlement were simply status quo and it was expected of me to be a participant in their schemes. Money came in from many directions, so why not grab up all you can was the unsaid prevailing perspective. I was just a little guy; these guys were big operators to me. They were bringing me up in the business and I could pick up a few crumbs along the way. You had to be one of them though. It was communicated to me early on that there were certain groups of people drivers were not particularly welcoming of, much of that changing in the ensuing years. Women were not exactly well accommodated for as drivers for a long time. That changed. Those who were anything other than straight in sexual identity were not exactly being provided shoes to put on, at least not in driver's union, but that changed as the pendulum eventually swung the other direction. What has never changed, however, is the explicit disdain a vast number of individuals in that business hold for people of the Christian faith. In all the time I spent working in showbiz, I met and worked alongside many, many people. Among that figure the sum total of Christians who revealed their faith to me is probably about a dozen. Sure, there were likely a few more, some whom I was simply unaware of, but if you are a Christian who wants to continue working in Hollywood, then you had better keep your mouth shut. Despite all that and as a result of divine orchestration, one of my dearest friends I have today is a Christian man I met while working in the industry. I introduce my friend Rob in the next chapter.

Submitting receipts for reimbursement for anything and everything progressed into something that I began to consider not very dignified in my way of thinking. The same could be said of other involvements, including padding paychecks. I initially held no objections, especially when there was something involved in it for me. It had been requested of me to obtain whatever receipts I could. Some stated figures higher than the actual expense while others represented an expense that was never actually incurred. Kickbacks were tempting, but came at a compromise of integrity, at least increasingly so for me. There was equipment that had long been broken down sitting there on rental. I saw a single fuel truck on rental on at least two shows simultaneously. Was that really okay to do or was it rather a matter of just bending the rules a little? I personally witnessed various items placed on rental under the condition that a portion of the money, sometimes up to one-half, was returned in cash. This was not only transportation equipment, but anything associated with a production. Four large portable AC units were billed for, but only two were actually there. Paychecks were issued to individuals who were family or friends, but they were seldom or never present. Sometimes that was only for a day or a for few days, but I have seen it continue on for weeks and months. All that was besides those few extra hours added onto a timecard here and there. The fact is, I could go on and on describing these things.

During my time working as craft service and assistant stage manager on *Tales* I was using my own pickup truck. Besides commuting to and from work, I would use it to shop for groceries daily, transport equipment as needed, and also to go on location with the production company. Not having much experience under my belt, I was unfamiliar with standard procedures in the industry regarding the use of personal equipment. The customary process in employing craft service includes compensating the person for use of their equipment. Any vehicle utilized for the purposes of executing their required tasks is placed on rental with the production company, the employee receiving a weekly dollar amount for that piece of equipment. In like manner various tables, ice chests, chaffing dishes, utensils, etcetera owned by the craft service person are also compensated for as a package deal referred to as a box rental. Possessing no prior knowledge or experience, I was completely unaware of these things. As it was, I felt I was actually getting something at the time. My boss was returning to me one half of the amount of any fuel receipt I submitted to him in cash. One day I was approached by my boss's transportation captain and co-captain, informing me that my truck was on rental and my boss was collecting the check. Not long thereafter, one of the night guards who was cleaning the offices on a nightly basis while simultaneously performing his guard duties discovered a document on our boss's desk. Showing it to me, it revealed the truth about what those guys had told me. The accounting office paperwork specifically showed my pickup truck as being on rental and listed my boss as the recipient of the proceeds. When I brought the subject up with him, he replied by suggesting I have a job that I should be happy to have, hinting that perhaps it could be otherwise. To that, he added my truck was insured with the company, an implied benefit to me. He further proposed that I could make up the difference by turning in even more fuel receipts for which I would receive half of the face value. From what I can tell, my truck was on rental all along for at least a year prior and at least another thereafter. His concessions did not end there: I was offered additional weekend shifts as guard/office cleaner, something I had already been doing.

For about the first year of doing craft service, all the purchases being made in performing my duties went through my boss. Buying food, beverages, and supplies produced a small stack of receipts daily. Unbeknownst to me, I should have had petty cash issued from the accounting office directly to me and I would then be required to submit receipts to them. Everything changed when I was called into the accounting office and was asked to provide an explanation for certain expenses claimed for craft service. A grocery store receipt indicated the purchase of hair conditioner, an item not used in the process of carrying out the duties of craft service. Although this was the first time it had been addressed with me, apparently it happened before and the potential of me retaining my job was in jeopardy because of it. Scrutinizing that lengthy receipt, we observed the purchase was made on a weekend and in San Bernardino which just happened to be where my boss lived some 75 miles away. I was subsequently exonerated of any wrongdoing and from that day on petty cash was issued directly to me.

I continued to work most weekends, usually three 12-hour shifts, that being in addition to my 70 to 80 something weekday hours. Thankfully, the weekends were quiet and easy. At some point between Saturday morning and Sunday night a cleaning lady would come in to clean the offices. The weekend guard assisted her in those chores, not bearing the entirety of the responsibility as was the circumstance with the guard shifts at night throughout the week. Although I did appreciate having that job, the other guards and I found ourselves somewhat irked when the reality of the situation became exposed. Another document had been discovered on our boss's desk indicating a cleaning company had been issued checks all along for five office cleanings per week. That company? Our boss's own mother.

Somewhere around 1990 I made the purchase of a 1-ton dually pickup truck I thought I would be able to send out on rental. There were two or three other leads I had at the time besides my boss. After contacting them, they all conditionally required from me a portion returned in the form of a cash kickback. Regretting the acquisition, I ended up selling the truck to my boss at a lesser price than what I had paid for it. Placing it on rental himself, he encountered a series of issues with the truck which required a number of repairs. I know that at least some, likely all of these expenses were submitted as transportation department expenses to the production accounting department, therefore he avoided assuming the cost himself. It was told to me that one of those mechanical failures required a complete engine rebuild. That breakdown happened when the show was on location in the desert North of Los Angeles at El Mirage dry lakebed. My boss's transportation captain had several pieces of his own equipment on the show, all under that same conditional requirement of a kickback. This man was one of the leads I had when I bought the 1-ton truck, but now he himself had become subjected to the same tangled web of shenanigans that go on. Upset about the working relationship he had with his transportation coordinator, he vandalized the truck I sold my boss by putting sand in the radiator when they were on location at El Mirage.

The fact of the matter is that all these extracurricular activities, although at one time providing a little something extra for me, evolved into something I viewed as morally objectionable. These things ran contrary to the moral dictates of my Christian faith. Where else was I to go? What other occupation could provide the income potential showbiz held for me? As I considered the possibilities, the realization came that whatever I went on to do had to be meaningful. According to my conscience, the product of my labors had to provide greater benefit to myself and to others than what I had been doing for the previous six or seven years. That is what led to my decision to pursue a career in healthcare. I decided to become a registered nurse.

That first half of 1992 proved to be yet another event filled season on *Tales from the Crypt*. In late May of that year I married the lady I had been with for the previous year and a half. We moved from Southern California, out of Los Angeles to San Luis Obispo. This area of the Central Coast of California was her hometown. It was where her parents resided and where I would ultimately continue my education. Up to that point I did not make it into the union. In the big picture of things there was something I had yet to realize: God's plan. I spent nearly seven years residing in San Luis Obispo. Specific circumstances would eventually and unyieldingly steer me those 200 or so miles back south to Los Angeles where showbiz was calling out to me, "Come back, kid!"

CHAPTER 7

THE COMEBACK KID

The LORD said to him,
"Go back the way you came......."

1 Kings 19:15a

But one thing I do: Forgetting what is behind and
straining toward what is ahead, I press on toward the goal
to win the prize for which God has called me
heavenward in Christ Jesus.

Philippians 3:13b-14

I BEGAN MY college education in the Los Angeles area. When I
moved to the Central Coast of California in May of 1992, I transferred
schools and continued my studies there. I worked a short time as a
certified nursing assistant to gain experience in healthcare and I also
completed training as an emergency medical technician. My wife, a
nurse herself, began to form the opinion that perhaps I should take
up a different career. My grades were very good, but a variety of circumstances were steering me another direction. I had discovered the
commercial fishing industry operating in the area and began to work

there some as well. I also continued to receive calls offering work in the motion picture industry. Although I turned down most of them, there were two I accepted, the production schedules conveniently coinciding with my school breaks. Working those two Summers, I stayed in Los Angeles during the week and made the 200-mile trek home on weekends. My wife sure appreciated the bump-up in our income and so did I.

In 1994 I received one of those calls. My friend Derek, who I got into the business, was doing craft service on a feature film and was requesting my assistance. F.A. Miller being the production manager provided additional incentive. Temperatures soared into the 100 and teens that July as we labored through those typical long filming days on the soundstage, this one an airplane hangar at Van Nuys Airport. Well into the project I was approached by F.A. informing me that the production was going union and in no uncertain terms he would see to it that I could enter the respective union local of my own choosing. Affording a person the opportunity to put their shoes on in Hollywood is no menial offering. I thought a lot of F.A.; he always treated me well and it was clear he held a strong appreciation for me also. Giving me the choice of any trade, I could jump from craft service to whichever – truly a generous offer. It was immediately evident my response had disappointed my friend. Just a few years prior I had obtained a class A driver's license in pursuit of Teamsters Union Local 399 membership. With a little more than a hint regarding his sentiments toward that group, F.A. would rather have seen me make a choice other than what I verbalized to him that day. He let me know that if I were to change my mind, then I was welcome to come back and see him. Otherwise, he suggested I speak with the transportation coordinator and his captain, Lee, which was the only department on the show that was already union. F.A. did not approach me again to address the subject and I remained working as craft service at the time the show went union. Although I had an established working relationship with the coordinator, his captain Lee absolutely despised me. I tried to get along with the man, but to no avail. Lee's ill feelings and union leadership ties would be something that would come to haunt me a few years later.

At the end of 1997 I found myself in the process of a divorce and it was not particularly amicable. We had two young children and I had every intention of remaining the prominent father I had been since their births, but their mother had other ideas. Family and friends in the Los Angeles area repeatedly insisted upon my return, but in no matter of reasoning did I have any desire to do so. I continued to work and attend classes in San Luis Obispo throughout the following year. Then the family court, contrary to what was best for our children, allowed their mother to move away to Riverside California, 250 miles away while at the same time retaining primary custody. In the process I had begun to seek the Lord with a little bit more sincerity. I was wrestling with my fair share of challenges and did not possess the vision to see that the Lord had certain things for me to accomplish back in Los Angeles, things that were His divine call upon my life. Moving back there was something I had been adamantly opposed to. San Luis Obispo was a far more preferable place to reside and I had no intention of leaving, especially if that meant moving back to the big city. I was lacking in sensitivity toward God's direction and His Holy Spirit's prompting in my life. In retrospect, I clearly see there was a distinct reason the motion picture industry was not letting go of me. God had a plan and so did I – they just were not the same, at least not yet. Via a series of unfortunate events, His will prevailed. Hard lessons can certainly be extremely unpleasant, but God will reach us one way or another when He has a plan for our lives. If you doubt that, then just read about Israel's forty years of wandering in the desert or about Jonah and his journey to Nineveh. Perhaps you too have learned a lesson from God the hard way, then looked back several years later in fond appreciation for what you now recognize as His loving guidance upon you as His dearly loved child. Not too long thereafter, I found myself moving back to Los Angeles and returning to the motion picture industry. I finally found myself engaging God's direction, traveling the path He laid out before me.

In October 1998 I made the move. Learning that Universal Studios was hiring drivers, a way some people attempt to get into the studio driver's union, I applied, interviewed, and was hired. After training, I tested and made it on as a tram tour driver. By the end of the Summer in 1999 I had met all the requirements and became a member of the union, Teamsters Local 399, the Hollywood Studio Drivers. I completed the required 30 days worked within a specified time period, paid a hefty initiation fee to the union local, and was sworn in. Besides driving backlot tram tours at Universal, I was then free to go to work as a union driver on productions. The time had come; I was finally putting my shoes on – some real, decent shoes or so I thought.

As 1998 was coming to a close, I had another plan in the works. With the opening of a new year, Rolling Dumpsters was all set up and operating in January of 1999. Borrowing several thousand dollars from my dear friend Delbert, I began with the purchase three hydraulically operated steel dump trailers and a 30-year-old pickup truck. Identifying a need in the industry, I carved out my own niche. As Johnny-on-the-spot, no garbage hauling business around provided the prompt response times I did. Quality of service takes precedence over price to meet the demands of showbiz. I had the trailers custom manufactured to meet the specifications used by drivers in the industry. Once the units were delivered, transportation could hook up and move them as needed with their own trucks. The Rolling Dumpsters trailers had approximately three times the holding capacity as the trash dumpsters that were being used. Long before my debt to Delbert was due, I had the entire loan paid off. I then borrowed another sum of money from him and acquired additional trailers, a process that would be repeated until I eventually owned a small fleet. In 2001 I bought a brand-new truck and added another in 2003. By this time Rolling Dumpsters Incorporated had become the leading provider of trash bins for television and movie productions on location in Los Angeles.

Throughout Scripture there are several instances wherein God prearranged meetings by divine appointment. Whether it is between a manifestation of Himself and a specific person or an orchestrated engagement between certain individuals, organizing rendezvous is just one of the many ways He works in our lives. That is just who He is and I am very thankful, having been an attendee at number of these occasions myself. I think we all have been at one time or another, we just do not realize it, at least not right away. The very first Rolling Dumpster I delivered went out to a beach house location where one of Aaron Spelling's television shows was being filmed. It turned out that the assistant location manager I met there was a Christian. Rob continued to use Rolling Dumpsters throughout the duration of its existence. I watched as it did not take long for him to advance from assistant to key location manager. God blessed Rob over the years with a wonderful wife and two boys who are now grown. I have been blessed to spend quality time with this beautiful family and have become well acquainted with them. As brothers in Christ, Rob and I have grown in our faith together, growing in love for God and for one another. His family and I have become very close and it will remain that way for all eternity. Divine appointments! This is clearly demonstrative how our loving Lord cares for His own. Thank you, Lord Jesus.

Although I was enduring an ugly custody battle, things were beginning to look up for me at that time. As a union driver in the industry I stood to prosper considerably. The business I started would have provided for me even significantly more so. Between the two, the sky was the limit. I was on track to become a very wealthy man. It took me a while, but I had finally gotten onboard with God's plan; I was beginning to see at least that much for myself. What I did not foresee, however, was the purpose of God's plan. He was not about to reveal that to me. If He did, then I would have proceeded an entirely different direction. The paths I would be required to forge through involved some pretty dark places. There was no way of knowing the extreme adversities that lay directly ahead.

CHAPTER 8

I HEARD IT WITH
MY OWN EARS

I heard, but I did not understand. So I asked,
"My lord, what will the outcome of all this be?"

Daniel 12:8

THAT RAINY NIGHT at Franklin Canyon Reservoir I learned a few things about the intentions of a far-reaching organized objective. As the years following transpired, I was informed even more on such matters. According to them, they are able to carry out their objectives bringing tremendous harm to their targets utilizing existing laws while affording themselves protection under those same laws. They spoke about how laws can be bent a long way without actually breaking them. This was besides the things described to me that were clearly criminal acts. All of it really did not make much sense to me, but it was on that rainy night when it was emphasized to me for the first time that this collaborative is far-reaching, connected extensively, powerful, and possesses an ultimate objective of achieving uncontested control. It seemed so far-fetched; I did not take them seriously. I considered that maybe they had done a few little things to a few people here and there, but as it turned out I had tremendously underestimated them. In no way were they exaggerating, not in the least. Athough something within me perceived it as inherently wrong, I possessed some degree of admiration for them at the time.

In this chapter I share much of what I was told, things I heard directly with my own ears. A large portion I recall entirely verbatim and am able to quote directly. There is also a fair amount that, although I remember the gist of what was being communicated, precise word for word recollection eludes me. In the interest of accuracy and continuity, I articulate the basic premise foregoing the use of quotation marks. Commentary is provided following each segment to help put it into context and to facilitate a better understanding.

<u>POTENTIAL LAWSUITS</u>

Nobody ever dares to sue us. If someone finds out that we're doing something to somebody they know, then we'll make a settlement agreement with that whistleblower person without telling the person we are after. The secret offer will be so generous that they just cannot refuse it. The agreement will be to set aside the money in its own special account. We'll agree to a set of conditions that have to be met for the subject to receive the money, but they will be conditions we will be able to keep from happening. The subject eventually knows something is going on, but they don't know exactly what. They'll have a camera so far up their @$$ we will know every single thing they're doing and they won't know what to do.

We will destroy the relationship between the subject and the whistleblower. We will divide them from their own family and friends and we'll use their own money to do it. They will be isolated and all alone, not trusting anybody. Some of them even commit suicide. Either that or they do something to retaliate somewhere. We've seen them do it against their own people. Then they'll end up in jail for it and we'll even get to them there.

The subject goes crazy and they end up dead, in jail, or move far away. They end up appearing to be absolutely nuts because the combination of the poison that messes up their mind and all the crazy stuff going on around them. Because they are acting angry and crazy, we get our politicians to take the money from that secret settlement account and then we start using it against them. The money will make its way back to our own people, the ones that we send to do things to them.

If there is a lawsuit in progress, then there are certain things we're not supposed to do, so we have to be careful. Once we've made a secret settlement though, then there is no lawsuit and we have a lot more room to work. After we destroy the relationship, the whistleblower ends up dead from a heart attack or a stroke. Then the person will never be able to hold them accountable for what happened; there will be nobody left for them to sue. The money and their dear friend will be all gone. Their whistleblower friend will be dead; how do you sue a dead person?!

The politicians that help us end up having a vested interest because so many bad things have happened. They've got skin in the game. Now they have to cover for themselves too.

By the time it ever gets into court, if they ever do get the money, they'll never be able to keep it because there'll be so many lawsuits flying around, they'll lose it all anyway. In the end there will be so much damage that there will be no possible way to pay for it all. If anyone tries to help them in any way, especially when it comes to a point where they might be getting close to receiving the settlement money, then we'll sue the person helping them. They cannot receive help; we'll back them off and it causes even more division between people.

These are just some of the things I learned that night at Franklin Canyon Reservoir. I wondered at the time just how truthful they were really being. I figured that maybe they had done some of these things they described to me, but certainly they had to be exaggerating, right? Afterall, this *is* showbusiness. These guys, I thought, were nothing more that big-talkers. In my mind they simply aspired to be some kind of highly revered bigshots like so many others chasing dazzling dreams in Hollywood. In the course of time, however, I found out they really do these things to people. Harsh reality came as far more than just a slap in the face when I later experienced these very weapons being used against me. I assure you, there was absolutely no exaggeration involved in their tales.

FROM EVERY ANGLE

If we are going after somebody, we come at them from every angle possible, not just face-to-face in court. When we have somebody in court, they'll start complaining to the judge that all kinds of bad things are happening to them outside of court. It goes on for a while and when they continue to bring it up, we'll say that we have nothing to do with it and suggest that they shouldn't be blaming us. When it continues, we warn them if they don't stop trying to pin those things on us, then we'll hold them accountable. It never stops and we sue them for slander. We get to the people around them: neighbors, friends, and even their family. Everybody has a price, some just cost more than others. We divide people. They will be losing friends all over the place. We'll have someone screwing his sister and she'll be giving us all kinds of information.

We would like to think that contained within the close-knit nature of our families there exists an impervious insulation against horrible things the world and the devil throws at us. As you will go on to learn in the following chapters, many of the very things I am exposing here eventually become weapons used against me. I really would have considered it otherwise impossible, but them getting to my family is among the countless adversities I have endured. I learned that my older sister became involved with a 399 driver she met online. In the days and weeks prior I had been warning her about these things, evidently to no avail. I felt fortunate because whatever was going on between them ended up being short-lived. That proved to be utterly insignificant compared to what occurred with my younger sister though.

In early 2013 Christopher Dorner, a former officer with the Los Angeles Police Department, went on a rampage in Southern California committing a series of shootings, killing four people and wounding three others. Following a nine-day manhunt, law enforcement officers got into a holdout with Dorner who had barricaded himself inside a mountain cabin northeast of Los Angeles. The structure erupted in a blaze consuming the cabin in flames. Once recovered, Dorner's charred remains were shown to have sustained a self-inflicted gunshot wound to the head. The series of tragic events had the entire nation captivated as we monitored national news media broadcasts watching it unfold. This was a little bit more than just another terrible news story to me. My younger sister, whom I will go in to more detail about in chapter nine, told me that she knew Dorner and that he was a "nice guy." She gave a veiled description about undercover work he was doing and appeared to be alluding to me in the process. In response to my questioning, she would not confirm or deny anything. I was simply left with her suggestion that perhaps I was a target of Dorner's investigatory activities. If that was the extent of what I had heard or had been through, then I would have lent absolutely no credence to what she was telling me. These events concerning Dorner, however, occurred directly on the heels of a near-death experience I suffered which is detailed in chapter 10. Although I cannot make a definitive correlation provided limited information, the Dorner situation coupled with what I was hearing from my younger sister evidences a fitting narrative to the disturbing things I heard with my own ears.

As you read on you will see I had a number of loved ones who could not be bought; they remained loyal to the relationship we shared. A few of them are gone now and for several others, the surrounding circumstances are more than just suspicious. By all human reasoning, I should not still be here myself. But God!

THE NETWORK

We've all got to stick together. There is power in numbers. We have to work together with all the other unions. When they go on strike, we will always honor their picket lines and they will honor ours, not just in the industry, but all unions.

We are connected all over with people at the top: the unions, police, politicians, and judges. We're all in each other's back pockets. If one of these people has a friend or family member that needs a good job, we'll get them one. Some members of our own union have family, sons or nephews or whoever, that are in gangs. We'll pay them off to do some dirty work and there's no way it can ever be traced because it's layered back too many people to make any connection to us. Things need to be layered back at least three or more people to cover our tracks.

If the federal government gets involved, then we will sue to back them off, unless our man is in the White House. State and local laws take precedence over federal laws. Once the court orders the feds to back-off, then that opens up the door for us to really go after people. All these things take time. If our man is in the White House, then we'll work with the feds.

It takes time to get things done. We can't do too many bad things to a person over too short of a period of time. We need to spread things out over time. That also helps us to get the right people in the right places.

Initially I found most of these things to be far-fetched, but these guys were quite serious. When a production is on location there are law enforcement officers on-set, often some regulars who work solely on shows. Those officers unionized coming under the Teamster's 399 Local even though these are uniformed law enforcement officers employed with various municipalities throughout Los Angeles and already have their own respective unions. Some said that was a union power grab, a claim one would be hard-pressed to refute.

> We have secret police that go after people. We get anybody we want investigated by the state. All kinds of crazy things start happening to them. They'll be getting poisoned while they're being investigated. The police wouldn't poison anybody! Remember, everybody has their price. Some just cost more than others. Stay away from them; they're being investigated.

The warning to stay away from people who are under investigation was adamantly asserted. They may be your friend or somebody you like, but if you are around them when something bad happens, then you could be a victim of collateral damage. To avoid a potentially fatal mistake, these guys emphasized avoiding targeted individuals. It did not take me long to realize that was precisely why certain people began to separate themselves from me.

My friend Jeff and I witnessed some kind of police raid being prepared one evening in the foothill community of Tujunga which is located in the Los Angeles suburbs near where we lived. We had just picked up dinner and drove over to a bank where I was going to use the ATM. We were sitting in my pickup eating in the empty bank parking lot and watched as a couple of cars drove in and parked next to each other behind the building, clearly making an attempt to be discrete. The drivers exited their vehicles and gathered together, conversing with several others who arrived shortly thereafter. Jeff and I watched with curiosity as they passed around some kind of paperwork, each one looking it over carefully before passing it on to the next person. Then they returned to their cars, opened the trunks, and began pulling things out. They were dressing themselves with holsters, firearms, and badges along with vests marked "Police." All of them then poured into the bed of a small, dark-colored minitruck and drove off, taking just that one vehicle bound towards what appeared to be a police raid. Jeff and I figured it had to be a drug bust. There were no uniformed officers and no helicopter was circling above. No additional support vehicles of any kind were around anywhere to be seen. We searched television and newspapers over the next few days, but found absolutely nothing about what we had seen. Jeff and I began to suggest perhaps they were not even actual law enforcement officers. Around that same time there were news reports about some kind of police groups conducting busts, confiscating drugs and money, but not taking any suspects into custody. Local government officials and police leaders had publicly released statements indicating these raids were likely being done by actual officers, but they were doing it on their own, outside of the context of legitimate law enforcement operations. The rogue cops had evidently banded together in gangs and proceeded to execute their own form of law enforcement. Jeff and I were never able definitively determine what we witnessed that evening, but it may well have been this scallywag consortium in action.

When it was said, "The police wouldn't poison anybody," it was verbalized with a mocking sarcasm accompanied with abundant snickering. Not knowing how to respond to such a claim, I was pretty much in disbelief. I really found that quite troubling and I earnestly trust that as you read this, you do too. Certainly not all law enforcement officers go along with these diabolical endeavors. The fact is that law enforcement is essential to law and order within any society. We need them. I choose to believe that most individuals employed in that profession operate with dignity, although I do have reservations in specific application to California and its large metropolitan areas. Wayward cops nonetheless make news headlines throughout the nation seemingly with increasing frequency. Police officers are in fact human beings. Although typically held in higher esteem than the civilian population, they are in no way exempt from the corruption that tempts every human being. Considering the potential for personal gain and the opportunity to wield authority over others, one can perhaps too easily be overcome by the temptations faced in this profession. In light of the political climate we are currently enduring, waywardness is not limited to individually misguided cops – entire agencies have engaged a "culture of corruption," as Jim McDonnell, the former Los Angeles County Sheriff himself stated. Polarized politicians and unions dictate the policies and procedures officers are required to adhere to. Abraham Lincoln once said, "Nearly all men can stand adversity, but if you want to test a man's character, give him power." The statements made by these two respectable men find disquieting specificity in application to individuals and institutions far beyond law enforcement. Current events in America demonstrate the consequences of evil run rampant.

THE ORGANIZED OBJECTIVE

Between all the people we have working together, the unions, the police departments, politicians, and judges, we pretty much have California locked up. We are going to take over the country. The main thing standing in our way are Christians, especially evangelical Christians.

I first heard these things said that rainy night at Franklin Canyon Reservoir. Lending the statement absolutely no credence, I considered it an absurdity at best. It was repeated a few more times over the ensuing years, but when I heard that first time, I was young and really did not care much about politics. What I believed at that tender young age was whoever happened to be in office did not carry much impact on how things operated in society; I figured everything went on just the same regardless. The passing of several years brought to me the realization these guys meant business; they actually were quite serious in what they were telling me. As Christians, we have been innocently unaware of this, but I am sounding out the alarm here and now. It is without question that what we see taking place in America today is the culmination of this objective. Their conspiring scheme has been in the planning stages for a long, long time. By the time I was being molded into one of their cronies, their craft had already become well-developed; it was nothing new.

TOXIC ENVIRONMENT

Break open batteries – they have to be alkaline batteries. Put it in food that has a strong flavor to mask it, like spicy food or coffee. They will end up with sudden and mysterious gut pains. They will receive a diagnosis saying it's being caused by food allergies, or lactose intolerance, or irritable bowel syndrome, or diverticulitis, or something else. Once there's a doctor's diagnosis, that opens the door for us to keep going and doing more, even using other poisons. We have a poison that affects the brain, it makes people act very angry. They go crazy and appear to be mentally ill. One of the poisons we use is uranium. We have to use just a little bit each time over a period of time, not too much at once. They will get rare and aggressive forms of cancer. Whatever happens to them from the uranium can take weeks or even months; it's slow acting, very long-acting. They will never be able to figure out where it came from. People sometimes think they're being poisoned, but the police wouldn't poison anybody.

There were a few people I worked with in the motion picture industry who faced certain health challenges related to gastrointestinal problems. I have personally known a few who wrestled with mysterious effects from a seemingly unknown affliction. Early on I had not made any connection in my own mind, but looking back I realize some of them were people that were not exactly sympathetic towards drivers and their union.

One of those people was F.A. Miller's own sister. She was the production coordinator on *Tales from the Crypt* and dealt with chronic abdominal pain. Somehow it was determined she suffered from lactose intolerance. The transportation captian who was involved in the Ipecac adulterating adventures absolutely abhorred her and was quite vocal about it. It would not have been difficult for him or someone acting on his behalf to access the small refrigerator near her desk in the front office.

Another guy I worked with, a soundman, expressed to me he was not particularly fond of drivers himself. It was from him that I first heard of the digestive disorder diverticulitis.

Still another man in the industry whom I befriended produced nonunion projects. He too was battling unknown digestive ailments. On one occasion he said to me, "If I were you, I'd get as far away from those people as I could get."

Drawing a distinct connection between these individuals and poisoning perpetrators is difficult. The health-related challenges I have described can and do occur outside of the realm of being criminally induced. Then again, considering each one of these people held a patent lack of esteem for drivers and their union, they may well have been the unwitting recipients of Satan's fiery darts.

I think it is far too easy to underestimate Satan. That ancient foe has many deviant, powerful, and wealthy people more than willing to do his bidding. The devil is the ultimate source of all these things and it his objective to steal, kill, and destroy (John 10:10). The more one stands with Christ, the greater threat we are to the adversary and the more he will make an effort to steal, kill, and/or destroy in us anything he possibly can. The devil is real, he is very active, highly destructive, and is intent on taking God's people down, inclusive of our entire country. 1 Peter 5:8 tells us, "Be alert and of sober mind. Your enemy the devil prowls around like a roaring lion looking for someone to devour." The reason I am writing this book is to shed light on such things, hopefully facilitating a new and greater spiritual visual acuity among our populace. This information needs to be told; it must be heard. These evil activities have been going on for a long time – far too long. I am doing and will do everything I can to expose it. It is imperative that the American people become aware of this evil stalking about us and we must respond accordingly against it. My intention is to put a face on the enemy, the face it is desperately and fiercely attempting to conceal. We are told in the Gospel of John, "Everyone who does evil hates the light, and will not come into the light for fear that their deeds will be exposed. But whoever lives by the truth comes into the light, so that it may be seen plainly that what they have done has been done in the sight of God" (John 3:20-21). The verse immediately preceding, verse 19, reads, "This is the verdict: Light has come into the world, but people loved darkness instead of light because their deeds were evil."

I asked many questions about the workings of the agenda, but it was evident I was not supposed to be so inquisitive. Typically my inquiries were not well accommodated, but at times I did receive some answers. One answer was given to me regarding the methodology of actually getting poison into a person. They found out where a person liked to eat. Any frequented establishment is considered a prospective opportunity. I was told fast food is an easy place to nail a victim. When I asked why I was told, "Do you know how much the people working there make?" "Minimum wage," I replied. That was the point exactly. They rationalized that a person working in such a place could be paid-off at a significantly reduced price. In regards to certain specific food establishments, I have heard it said, "We don't eat there." There was a particular emphasis on "We," implying one could potentially be subjected to collateral damage as an unintended victim.

Adulteration of food consumed at restaurants is by no means the only avenue utilized; it could occur with food in the home as well. While a targeted individual is away from home, they could get in. Not disturbing a single thing and leaving no evidence of an intruder, the victim's refrigerator and cupboard stores are easy prey. Furthermore, it was described to me how a prop used on a show might require customized manufacturing. An item could be tailor made in a factory for special reasons needed for filming. I was told workers at a given factory might just happen to be union and a good possibility too those transporting the products to market. Until I learned better, I thought these stories were just one whooper after another. Bearing them in mind, there is nonetheless a myriad of possibilities for nefarious opportunities all along the supply chain. These workers of iniquity can and do deliver their wares in any way possible. If in our own thinking we limit them to one single technique, then we only render ourselves all the more vulnerable.

I stated it earlier and it certainly bears repeating: It is far too easy to underestimate Satan. This is no walk-in-the-park spiritual battle for any child of God alive in the world today. Although the adversary's objectives have not changed, his methods have. He has been refining his craft over a long, long period of time. Having been stymied by God and his people time and again, that ancient foe is determined not to be frustrated yet again. He knows the Word of God quite well and is aware that his time here on earth is growing short, therefore he and his multitude of demons along with those he has conspired with to do his bidding are working diligently against God and His anointed. Yes, the final outcome has already been secured. Yes, as children of Light, we have been given authority over darkness. However, as long as we occupy an earthly tent and live in this fallen world, confrontation with darkness will be fierce. This being said, it is incumbent upon me to inform you that they are coming after us. Christians are being poisoned as we are a restraining force against evil in the world today and we must become aware. It does not matter one iota how you perceive me. Maybe you think I am the one telling tall tales. This is a harsh reality and I am warning you right here and right now. Many Christians have unknowingly been slaughtered during the course of Satan's unfinished drudgeries. Way too many have fallen ill to the effects of a toxic substance nefariously introduced into their bodies. They have subsequently received a medical diagnosis identifying something which is merely a symptom completely different than the actual cause. Many have paid the ultimate price. Loved ones, it is time for us to collectively push back against these evils. In Jesus Christ we have been given authority over the devil. Let the Church arise! Let our enemies be scattered!

WITHIN REACH

Nobody is out of our reach. We can get to anybody. It doesn't matter if they are a celebrity living in a gated mansion or a powerful person somewhere else, we can get to any person. We'll find out about the people around them and find the right person who will get the job done for us. If anyone ever testifies against us in court and is placed in a witness protection program, we'll find them there too. Often times they are given a job in the federal government like a park ranger with the Forest Service. We'll find them there too.

When I became a driver in the industry, I took notice that actors and actresses regularly leave food items behind in their cast trailers which is, of course, a piece of equipment under the control and supervision of the drivers. At times these would even be expensive food items. Once left unattended in their trailer, such things were not consumed or taken home with them, but simply left behind. As drivers, it was among our responsibilities to properly maintain all trailers, cleaning them after use. On many occasions I was the one bagging up and throwing away these left-behind foods and beverages. Sure, most of them are wealthy and the value is insignificant to them. There are also likely some that do return and consume items left unattended, but why such reluctance? Why are they so apprehensive about it? Do they know something or maybe just have suspicions? Have they experienced something before themselves or seen it happen to others? Clearly there is a prevailing issue among many of them in regards to looking out for their own safety and understandably so.

CHURCHES, PASTORS
AND CHURCH LEADERS

During that discussion when I was first told, "We are going to take over the country," and that Christians are their main obstacle, they also talked about how they just loved to mess with pastors and church leaders. They described it as an entertaining game and how it is amusing for them to see a Christian being driven crazy. They talked about churches being vandalized and satanic symbols spray painted on the walls. There was talk of churches mysteriously catching fire. Some of the same things I described them doing to potential whistleblowers and their kept-in-the-dark subjects they would also perpetrate upon pastors and church leaders. They claimed to have taken down entire churches.

In chapters one and two I told of how I began attending church and started to work in in the motion picture industry at virtually the same time. In retrospect, it is clear for me to see that was something the Lord orchestrated. At that time I was young and was being pulled in two diametrically opposed directions. When these guys told me about the things they did to Christians, I conveniently concealed my faith in fear of their judgment. I thought about my pastor and the high esteem I had for him. Searching for a response that would avoid incriminating myself, a timid statement rolled off my lips: "I know a man who is a pastor. He's a good man and you wouldn't be able to do those things to him." I was absolutely astonished when they laughed in response to what I said. Not just one, but all of them together simultaneously broke out in mocking laughter. That timidity would not be so disabling to me today as it was back then, but it had me in its grip. I was not about to tell them, 'Well, I'm a Christian.' Remember, I was like the son they had taken under their wings. I was surprised by their laughter. One of them put his hand on my shoulder and provided an explanation: between the crazy things happening all around them and the poisons effecting their minds, they go crazy. According to what was said, the effects provoke the victims to extreme anger in the process. These guys, in pursuing something that is shear entertainment to them, enjoy the process of doing to ministers and church leaders the same things they do to people they target for more serious reasons. "We take down churches," my young ears heard in disbelief. That experience was extremely disturbing to me then and always will be. That was a little more than thirty years prior to the writing of this book and it was clear that entire process was something they were already well experienced at.

<u>TRAVEL</u>

When someone we're after is traveling, that's a perfect time to go after them. They're away from home and might feel safe. The thing is, they are unfamiliar with their surroundings and the people around them. That leaves them vulnerable for us to get them.

When I first heard this, I was in no way an experienced traveler. In fact, at that point I had never even flown on an airplane. In time I would become personally acquainted with this subject. I describe in detail in chapter 10 how one of my best friends, Delbert, was the first voyaging victim. Then in 2012, when journeying to Central California I fell terribly ill myself. It would not stop there either. In 2021 I flew back to Los Angeles quite sickened after an incident in Bowling Green Kentucky.

<u>INVESTIGATIONS</u>

We can get anybody investigated. If a vendor in the industry comes around running a business without our approval, we'll have them investigated. Sooner or later something will be found on them and they'll get shut down. You have to have our permission to do business around here. Stay away from them, they're under investigation.

There was one particular instance wherein a man started a security guard business catering his services specifically to the industry. He had a noble idea in putting young people to work who had a troubled past and were attempting to get their lives together. It was unmistakably clear that many drivers and their union leadership did not like the man. The direction was given, "Stay away from him; he's being investigated." The informed knew well, any person around him could be subject to collateral damage. "Stay away," is good advice if you know any better. The man, his straw hat, and guard service were not around long. I am not sure what happened to him, but all of it seemed to just fade away into the past without any further mention of him or the circumstances.

<u>ELECTIONS</u>

Vote for this guy, he's our man. This is who we are voting for.

Whenever it comes time to cast a ballot for any election, union leadership informs the constituency exactly how to vote. I received literature from them in the mail and a call or two on the telephone as well instructing me in this regard. Never was I asked who I intended to vote for or what my opinions may otherwise have been. Without deviation, each and every time it was a matter of, "Who *we* are voting for." Everything was all prearranged: certain political candidates were to receive the unanimous votes of the unions inclusive of the entirety of their membership. One's own stance on issues or party affiliation were completely irrelevant. Each and every single candidate they partnered up with belonged to the Democratic Party, not once did I ever observe it to be otherwise. This all fits the narrative as described: "We pretty much have California locked up. We are going to take over the country." These cabals are all working conjunctively with concerted effort in pursuing the specific agenda of seizing absolute control and instituting oligarchical collectivism. This should provide an eye-opening awareness to us all. Look around the country today. Turn on the news broadcast and take a candid look at what is going on. Years ago it all seemed so far-fetched to me, but what we are currently experiencing is exactly what was communicated to me that 30-something years ago. It is also what I am attempting to communicate to you now. We desperately need a great awakening to save our nation as we know it. I love this country and I believe most people reading this do also. Failing to take notice and respond accordingly and appropriately entails only two real possible scenarios. Firstly, a person may, in all sincerity, be fundamentally deceived by this diabolical agenda. They therefore simply acquiesce to whatever trusted leadership demands of them. Contrarily, it is possible they are fully aware and thereby complicit. There are many Americans who hate this country, especially our Christian heritage and values. Regardless of the rhetoric spewing forth, their actions speak otherwise and it is becoming increasingly evident to a growing and discerning portion of the population. I firmly believe many will come to see through the smoke and mirrors, realize an awareness of what is actually going on, and alter their course. I have personally witnessed quite a few already. I myself may be counted among that number as well. It is my earnest prayer for the American people and for the entire world that we embark upon a new standard of righteousness, displacing these evils and their agenda. We the People are ripe for a great awakening. We need to look well beyond charming personalities and presumptuous societal ties when we approach the ballot box. We cannot persist in voting into office individuals associated with this agenda and continue to govern ourselves; they will end up governing us as is their ultimate objective. Lasting change can and must be made when we avail ourselves at each and every election. Furthermore, real change, that is lasting transformation, can only take place when we humble ourselves in sincere repentance before our Creator. This kind of change takes place in the human heart and is found nowhere else but in Jesus Christ. Changed lives possess the capacity to impact our entire society and usher in the change we so desperately need as a nation.

<u>MISCELLANEOUS</u>

We need time. It takes time to get to people. Be patient, it takes time. We've got to get the right people into place. We can't do too much in a short period of time. Things can't be too obvious; we've got to be able to cover our tracks. We layer things back at least three or more people, that makes it impossible to connect it back to us.

Use roofing nails under the tires. Throw a few on the ground so they run 'em over when they pull away. Always use roofing nails. They have a large head, so it makes them pop up into the tire tread when they're ran over. Put _____ in the diesel fuel tank. It only takes a little bit, like a quart or two for the whole tank. It will ruin the injectors and cause expensive internal engine damage. The truck will be blowing out huge clouds of white smoke. Even if they drain the fuel tank and look at the fuel, they'll never be able to tell it's there because it doesn't change the color of the fuel.

I do not recall exactly what the substance was they said they used to destroy diesel engines, but it is one of the chemical solvents found in the paint section in hardware stores, perhaps lacquer or lacquer thinner.

Sometime around 2004-05 my pastor and his wife purchased a house and I assisted them in moving into it. Thoroughly washing out one of my Rolling Dumpsters trailers, I utilized it and my pickup truck to transport their belongings from their rented apartment to their new home approximately seven miles away. After a long day of hard work they wanted to treat me to dinner at a nearby restaurant. Arriving with my truck and trailer, there was little room up close, so I had to park them at the far end of the lot. After returning an hour or two later, I started my truck and drove away. Traveling less than a mile, white smoke began coming out of the exhaust pipe. That rapidly increased to larger billows. Soon, huge clouds of white smoke were leaving a wake behind me and the engine began to sputter. I purchased the 2003 Ford diesel F-250 brand-new and it did not have a huge number of miles on it. When the dealership's mechanics addressed the problem, they were unable to identify exactly what caused the expensive internal damage. They drained the fuel tank and inspected the fuel, but that did not produce an answer either. It ended up costing me several thousand dollars.

When we mess with people, sooner or later they will strike back in some way, especially if they are a young man, and they will get caught and thrown in jail. We see everything they do. We see every move they make. They'll have a camera so far up their @$$ they won't know what to do.

Please excuse the language here; it is certainly not a colloquiallism emblematic of my vocabulary. I am simply repeating it to you as it was said to me. This is exactly what I heard and I am inerrantly conveying it to you.

In our divorce she got the business and I got the house. She ran the business into the ground. She didn't know what she was doing.

I once listened to a story a driver told about his experience going through a bitter divorce battle. His wife did not work in the industry as he did. In addition to being a union driver, he owned several trucks that were placed on rental on television and movie productions. When his equipment went out on a show, it was not from him as individual, but rather from the company he had formed to provide rental trucks to the industry. This is commonly the practice and can be a significantly profitable enterprise as it had been for him for several years. Throughout the marriage she personally observed the profitably of their business and shared in the spoils. In the divorce proceedings it was suggested she received the business which she perceived to be a producing goldmine. He conspired with his cohorts; it was a set-up from the start. Following negotiations she was granted ownership of that business. It was then for her to rent the trucks out to shows, shows on which union drivers rented and operated the equipment. Supposedly, a noncompeting contractual agreement had been signed by both parties in the process which is standard procedure in the business world. As long as she owned and operated the venture, he would be prohibited from taking part in any operation which would contend against her interests. As I mentioned earlier, the union boys talked about how they need time to accomplish their endeavors. This, however, did not take that long. As he told the story, she could not keep up with the necessary and increasingly numerous repairs in addition other unforeseen issues. He continued, "She ran it into the ground" within about two years. Subsequently, he was able to reestablish his equipment rental enterprise. Once his ex-wife's business was no longer in existence, he was afforded the freedom to reestablish the income stream for himself.

When I got pulled over and arrested for drunk driving, I called the union office. They came down and got me out. There was no court date or anything. That was the end of it.

This particular driver talked about how he had been pulled over after consuming alcohol, arrested, and hauled down to the police station. He did not bother to call a lawyer, his wife, nor a bail bondsman. He called the union! And that was that!

I know how to use a pocket knife,
I'm a Teamster.
Hollywood is a small town.

These things were said directly to me by Tony Cusumano, one of the former head honchos at the 399 Union Local. He said them when we met for lunch at the Smokehouse Restaurant in Burbank. We had been discussing the subject of my equipment being vandalized on shows, including a number of tires which had been slashed. My friend Derek had an acquaintance who worked closely with Tony and it was through him that he arranged for us all to meet for lunch. This meeting took place in 2000 or 2001 at a time when I was both running my business and working as driver. The equipment I sent out on shows was being increasingly vandalized at the time, that being just one of the issues I addressed with Tony during our lunch meeting. Being his own idea, Derek specifically arranged the occasion because he wanted them to see that "You're [I'm] a nice guy." Many of them, however, including Tony, really did not like me before and were certainly not about to grant me any kind of newfound favor. Tony inquired about my connections in the industry, wanting to know the people I knew and worked for. When I mentioned a production manager, F.A. Miller, whom I worked for and became friends with, Tony blurted out, "He's a sick f***er too!" The look on his face showed he immediately regretted that retort. Having said, "too," he was implying that was in addition to what he really thought about me. Tony's facial gestures spoke, 'I should not have said that,' but it proceeded from the depths of what was in his heart. It was as if he was futilely attempting to reel in a fish that was getting away; it was too late.

The comment Tony made about knowing how to use a pocket knife he said in the context of a discussion regarding how union members vandalize equipment belonging to those who operate without their approval. It was a veiled remark and alluded to what I was actually experiencing. "Hollywood is a small town," was a masked threat as well. In other words, we know everyone we need to know around here to get the job done.

You are crazy standing up to those guys. Dude, you're nuts! Are you okay?! They're going start messing with you and I don't want to be around when they do. How much can you take from those guys?!

One day on the set of the movie *Windtalkers,* I was busy going about my business picking up and delivering dumpster trailers. Nearby, a group of drivers were standing just outside the open door of a Star Waggons trailer where they were having a discussion with Leo Reed, head of the driver's union local. Among them was a guy I worked with at Universal Studios as tram tour drivers. The posse approached and proceeded to pepper me with questions, making suggestions regarding how Rolling Dumpsters should be subject to union dictates. Contrary to what they were telling me, I claimed that as owner of Rolling Dumpsters, I would make the decisions for the business. When one of them suggested I was crazy, I boldly asserted, "The power that is in me is greater than the power that is in this world!" Appearing somewhat perplexed, my response seemed to ascertain their conclusions about me. It was clear where their counsel had come from: I looked over at that Star Waggons trailer where the door was being held open just an inch or two and it suddenly closed shut.

As I continued to conduct my business over the next few years, I would hear similar things from drivers and location managers alike. It was my friend, Derek, whom I had gotten into the business several years prior, the one who arranged that lunch meeting with Tony Cusumano, that said to me "They're going to start messing with you and I don't want to be around when they do." His concerns were certainly not unfounded nor was he experiencing irrational fears. Derek has some knowledge about these guys and how they go about conducting business. He has more than half a clue regarding what they are capable of. It has been suggested to me that a true friend would not abandon another so readily. Otherwise a loyal friend, Derek undoubtedly weighed benefit versus risk in taking the approach he chose. He had valid reasons to be fearful, not only for himself, but for his loved ones as well. Derek knew he could become a victim of collateral damage and was willing to sever ties with me in the interest of self-preservation.

> What is your Social Security number? That is how we look up our members. Okay here you are, I found you. We have you on a list eligible for reinstatement.

Several years transpired after I should have ceased to receive any correspondence from the union office, yet voting literature continued to show up in my mailbox. For the most part, I simply consigned the pompous drivel to an appropriate rubbish receptacle. When their balloting material arrived in the mail one day, my curiosity got the best of me. I called the union office, identifying myself by name, and inquired why I continued to receive mail from them. After placing me on hold, the same female voice returned asking, "What is your Social Security Number? That is how we look you up, by your Social Security Number." Never having encountered that before when I was a member, I became suspicious, so I provided her a numerical quote nothing near accurate of my true SSN. She responding by saying something to the effect of, 'Okay I've found you right here.' That immediately substantiated my skepticism regarding the truthfulness of our conversation. They knew who was calling them, but why they wanted my SSN I do not know. Would they really need to identify whether or not they possessed personal record of any individual to provide an answer as to why they were sending union election literature specifically addressed to a nonmember? What I do know is that my conscience absolved me even though I had lied. Without obtaining my real SSN, they proceeded to explain they had me on a list as eligible for reinstatement into the union. It does not matter how lucrative the occupation or how much it offers to pay, I will never return to the yoke of pulling heavy burdens Hell-bound. Believe me, after experiencing many of their attempts to drag me into the pits of Hades with them, I have felt those terribly unpleasant flames lapping at me – they burn. A person should expect nothing less when the power of darkness comes in.

WHEN THE POWER OF DARKNESS COMES IN

Be alert and of sober mind. Your enemy
the devil prowls around like a roaring lion
looking for someone to devour.

1 Peter 5:8

IN THE PAST when I have heard men going through a divorce complain about how the courts were treating them unfairly, I usually deemed it as something they had brought upon themselves. I learned firsthand that these things can be very lopsided. The proceedings I had been enduring were seemingly without end as the family court proved themselves rather adept at serving up injustice. Sitting in the courtroom awaiting my turn, I watched at least one other man get the short end of the stick. I also observed quite a few other cases adjudicated during the numerous court dates I attended, but never did I observe elsewhere the obvious indiscretions I was subjected to. It felt as if I had been singled out and targeted. It appeared as if the judge was searching for the crime that would fit the punishment all within the so called "family court."

During one particular appearance I made before a judge, she inquired about my employment and income. I answered honestly of course, and then she asked if belonged to a union. When I told her that I belonged to Teamsters Union Local 399 Studio Drivers, she acted very excited, quickly and zealously scribbling with a pen. At that moment it seemed Lady Justice's blindfold had dropped from her eyes and the scales she held were being weighed sans impartiality. That judge appeared to be prosecutor, judge, jury, and executioner all in one – in the "family court."

On another occasion at the Riverside Family Court, we met with other staff members in some kind of mediation process. My intentions all along had been to peaceably resolve differences with the best interest of our children in mind. Never did I take an adversarial or antagonistic approach during our interactions, but that does not mean I was met with the same from others. When I was in conversation with the so-called unbiased mediator, the woman began accusing me of "speaking in code." In no uncertain terms, I desired to make my communication unambiguously clear and stated so to her, but she only repeated herself, "You're speaking in code." Although I assured her that was not my intent, a bias obviously existed and nothing I had to say was going to pacify her. I apologized saying, "I am sorry if you are having trouble understanding me or I am not making myself clear." Rephrasing my statements and answers to her questions had absolutely no effect in altering this individual's predisposition. Do I have trouble articulating my thoughts and communicating them clearly to others? Tell me, what do you think?

Not long after that, Rolling Dumpsters incidence of vandalized equipment snowballed. It is my firm belief that court made contact with my union. Those familiar words I first heard years ago echoed in mind once again: "We're all in each other's in back pockets – the unions, the police, politicians, and judges."

Even though I was enduring an onslaught of sabotage, Rolling Dumpsters volume of business steadily increased at the same time. In addition to establishing new contacts, I was reconnecting with familiar faces from the past, although some not so pleasant. One day when delivering a trailer, I saw a man I immediately recognized standing there staring straight at me. I pretended not to see him and it appeared he did not realize I had taken notice of him. It was Lee, whom I mentioned in chapter seven. My dumpster trailers collected a few union stickers along the way when they were out on shows and I added a few more myself. It evidenced that whoever owned this equipment held 399 loyalties. As I approached, Lee turned and began to speak with a man standing next to him. I jumped out of the truck quickly enough to hear Lee say, "How the hell did he get in?!" with a flabbergasted indignancy. That man hated me back in 1994 and he definitely did not care for me one bit then in 1999. I saw him around a few more times after that. As could be expected, my trailers returned from his shows damaged and defaced on a number of occasions.

As business continued to increase, so did the vandalism of my equipment. Initially, they were minor things like broken taillights or air let out of tires. I adapted quickly, promptly remedying minor issues. If that was the extent of it, then I could have continued indefinitely. That was not to be, however, as the damage inflicted became worse and worse. License plates were missing. Then a couple of years into business I discovered the license plates had been exchanged between all the trailers. Although I remedied the situation, swapped plates became a chronic issue. Electrical lines were completely rewired causing multiple blown fuses and electrical problems with the tow vehicles. An entire hydraulic unit was stolen. Then, after picking up a brand-new trailer and delivering it on a show, it was never to be seen again. It went directly from the manufacturer to a guarded filming location where it was stolen. The location manager on that show was one of the few good guys. He saw to it that I was fully and promptly compensated for the loss. That was merely the first of several trailers that would be purloined over the next few years. I received reimbursement for only one other, that coming as a result of a small claims court judgment.

In January of 2007 two Rolling Dumpsters were taken at one time from my equipment storage yard. Dozens of tractor-trailers used this same storage lot, each one a paying tenant required to lock the gate upon exiting. My designated area was at the far inside end of the long rectangular lot. As fate would have it, the lot manager happened to be a 399 Teamster himself. He did not respond kindly when I presented my dilemma to him. Although I had seriously considered civil litigation, he suddenly and unexpectedly lost his contract on the lot, undoubtedly costing him considerable income. He gave some strangely obscure verbal indication that I was somehow responsible for his lost lease. I certainly had no knowledge of the circumstances, although I cannot begin to dismiss the possibility that it was Divinely orchestrated. I went down to L.A.P.D.'s Foothill Division Police Station and filed a report. The officer just began taking the report when another uniformed officer walked in and began speaking with another cop in the back, the watch commander I suppose. I immediately recognized the one who walked in as the cop I had seen with Councilman Villaraigosa about three years prior. That commander guy then came out and relieved the officer who started writing the report, pulling out a completely different form. He then proceeded to take what I was led to believe was a stolen vehicle report for my two missing trailers. A few days later I received notice from the police department informing me one of those missing trailers was in their impound yard. After paying them a fee, I recovered the trailer which had sustained extensive vandalism. The second unit was never recovered.

On still another occasion, I had a trailer stolen from a guarded parking lot on a show. Filing a report at the Glendale Police Department, the document they gave me was titled, *Report of Stored Vehicle*. I immediately questioned that, but they assured me that was their standard report for stolen vehicles and they did not have my Rolling Dumpster stored. The production company was not readily willing to compensate for the loss, so I filed a case in small claims court and was subsequently awarded judgement, although at a reduced value based upon the judge's appraisal of the trailer's worth.

Although I had been facing more than my fair share of challenges, I was working diligently and experiencing a respectable measure of success. My plan was to eventually reach out to other industries with Rolling Dumpsters, growing and expanding the operation in a variety of ways. Looking forward, the potential was virtually limitless. I was being horribly assailed in the meantime, but was not fearful of those guys. People that knew better thought I was absolutely crazy, but I stood up to those clowns. It was indeed difficult to endure, but I persevered and persisted in working very hard. If that vandalism had remained limited to only equipment, then Rolling Dumpsters would have prevailed much longer than the nine years it was in existence. Wishful thinking I suppose that was; the vandalism progressed on to the bodies of human beings.

There are some very important reasons cops are employed on film shoots. When a piece of transportation equipment is being moved around, uniformed police officers are often needed to stop traffic. Working in the big city often involves heavy traffic and I have been very appreciative of their assistance on many occasions. Whether I was a driver on a show or a vendor delivering a Rolling Dumpster, their services have been an indispensable asset. Most of the time, delivery and pick up of my trailers would take place before and after officers or any crew were present at the location. When making a delivery while they were there, they would always lend help as needed. A few years into my business endeavor something changed. At first it was not so obvious. I would arrive at the designated place of delivery only to be completely ignored. Dismissing it as a minor oversight, I was perfectly capable of accomplishing the task on my own one way or another. This, however, became a regular experience over a relatively brief period of time. I would arrive with a delivery and await my turn. The officers were going about their duties assisting transportation, then turned and walked away at the point when they would otherwise be assisting me. The whole thing became blatantly obvious: Rolling Dumpsters was not to be included in the scope of their operations. I had not done anything to them. I had always respected and appreciated them. If I was guilty of a crime, then arrest me and hold me accountable, but that was not the case. It was evident some kind of directive had been issued against me and my business.

The enigmatic aversion I had become to some was in no way limited to the confines of working in the industry. What had its genesis there gradually became my experience elsewhere. Around that same time I had a number of encounters when a marked police car traveling past me the opposite direction made an abrupt U-turn, sped up quickly behind me, but did not initiate a traffic stop as they appeared to be doing. What were they after? After receiving this treatment from L.A.P.D., Los Angeles County Sheriffs, and C.H.P. alike, I was left wondering what I was wanted for that was so bad. If I had robbed a bank, then perhaps I would have thrown the stolen loot out the window when they came up behind me. There were no dead bodies in my truck or trailers; I had not killed anybody nor did I intend to. If I had been guilty of some grievous offense, then certainly I would have been deservedly arrested. None of this, however, was the circumstance.

All that came to a crescendo one day when I was driving along Foothill Boulevard near my home. A black and white L.A.P.D. squad car made an aggressive U-turn and accelerated hastily taking position directly arrear of me. After turning left at the next traffic signal, they continued to follow, so I pulled over to the right shoulder of the road. Not knowing really what to expect, I watched in my mirrors as the female officer driving the car, accompanied by her male companion, pulled to a stop behind me. Good, I thought. I had a few questions for them to answer. Their feigned actions of conducting a traffic stop abruptly shifted as they suddenly took off around me. I was in no way content to leave the matter at that, so I took off after them. As short-lived as it was, I found myself in a police chase. It was quite paradoxical: I was actually the one who was chasing them! I know the roadways in that community well. When she made a right turn two blocks up, I immediately recognized it as a dead-end street and continued in pursuit. Arriving at the end, the squad car circled around facing me, but I was blocking the road preventing passage. I placed the transmission in park as we were locked in a stare down for what seemed to be an eternity. No gestures were made by any of us. They did not exit the vehicle and approach me as I fully expected them to. I sat there for about a minute waiting for them to do something, anything! How crazy was that?! If I was suspected of wrongdoing, then just arrest me! I was obstinately determined not to tolerate their maltreatment any longer. Who were the real criminals involved here anyway? After realizing that was the extent of their genuine interest in me, I finally pulled up leaving enough room for passing. Seizing the opportunity, she floored the pedal, fleeing the scene of the crime as quickly as possible in the getaway car. From that day forward, whenever I encountered such things, I simply ignored them. They eventually ceased that odd approach to what was clearly something else dressed in the guise of law enforcement.

In vandalizing my equipment, mirrors on my trucks became the target on several occasions. One time I was driving along a main thoroughfare when another pickup traveling the opposite direction swerved toward me. I promptly moved to the right within my lane leaving enough room to safely pass, but the other driver made a second move at the last moment causing our driver's side mirrors to smash together. The dual maneuver made it clearly evident the collision was intentional and that was not the first time. It was, however, the first time I was able to obtain a license plate number. Making a U-turn at the first intersection, I quickly tracked down and followed the motorist while calling 911. After breaking off from trailing him, I met nearby with an L.A.P.D. officer who told me the man had supposedly done the same thing in several places in the recent past. About two weeks later I received a call from somebody identifying themselves as an L.A.P.D. officer offering monetary compensation for my loss. Nothing at all was said about insurance which would have been standard procedure. I was simply offered money by the police to pay for the damage. The whole situation reeked of a setup from the start. After similar dilemmas involving mirrors and considering other experiences with law enforcement, I did not trust them and simply did not respond. The whole thing was a farce from the get-go.

A couple of years after the great mirror adventure, another collision of sorts occurred not far from that same place. I was stationary at a red light when I watched a man drive up on my right side, come to a stop, and then creep up slowly into my right front fender. Again, the situation was deliberate. I could see the man's face the whole time; he was not distracted. After pulling off to the curb the man exited his vehicle, began shouting obscenities, and proclaimed I was going to pay for his car. I was certainly not going to respond in like manner and proceeded to take pictures with my cell phone instead. The fellow did not like that at all and started coming close to me, so I backed away. He continued to approach, still shouting and flailing his arms wildly, and I was feeling quite threatened. When I was a younger man, that may well have become a physical confrontation, but I had grown up a bit. Perceiving the entirety of the circumstances as a staged event, I suspect that was how I was expected to respond. I was not about to acquiesce and I was not about to get thrown in jail over the matter either. Having no confidence in a police response, I dialed 911 anyway. I described to the operator exactly what was taking place and that I was being threatened. At least half an hour passed as I kept my distance. From a distance, I repeatedly suggested to the man we exchange insurance information, but to no avail. After watching a police car casually drive past, I made the call again only to be told officers in the area were preoccupied. In all, I think I waited there about two hours. Nobody from the police department ever showed up at the scene and unlike the mirror caper, I received no follow-up call.

In major cities throughout the United States an ideology has arisen to defund police departments. It is a foolish point of view to say the least. Those who propose this approach would undoubtedly see things quite differently if they became the victim of a violent crime. What would a person do when they need the police in an emergency situation only to discover that resource does not exist? Taking into account all I have experienced with law enforcement in the Los Angeles area, that is the exact situation I have lived in for many years. To this day, law enforcement resources are something I virtually live without. There have been a few things I have witnessed over the past several years when I would otherwise have dialed 911, but did not. Like most people, I want to live in a safe community. I desire to know the cops and have a good working relationship with them – to support what they do and to respect each other. Because I did not bow down and worship at the altar of the almighty union, this concept has proved elusive. I have borne the brunt of that decision and it has cost me considerably. Perhaps someday I will reside in a different part of the United States, a place where better things will be my reality.

Besides these crazy things on the road, I watched as a friend of mine was framed in a vehicle accident in front her home while I just happened to be working there. That too was precalculated and once again people arrived at the scene attempting to incite violence. On and on it goes, one injustice after another. I once sat in a courtroom as a uniformed California Highway Patrol officer gave false testimony under sworn oath. In the courthouse corridors later, I called him a liar. He did not like that. He exclaimed, "I don't appreciate being called a liar!" which only prompted me to reiterate the truth. "Liar!" I countered. There is so much more I have not mentioned here; it goes on and on, one injustice after another. Although civilians should have confidence in the justice system, I do not and it grieves me. Even after what I have been through, I find the suggestion we would be better off without law enforcement a complete absurdity. I have lived it; believe me loved ones, you do not want to. It is a vital constituent of a virtuous and orderly society. I will state it like this: defunding the police is a satanic ideology. Lawlessness will, after all, pave the way for the Man of Lawlessness, the Antichrist himself (2 Thessalonians 2:1-12).

In October of 2001 I was visiting with my friend Delbert in his home when a pop sound interrupted our conversation. I simultaneously felt an acute sting on the side of my head and caught a glimpse of a small object falling to the carpet. Observing what had just occurred, a BB had been shot from outside right through a window and was laying on the floor next me. I immediately ran outside and witnessed a dark blue BMW with dealership license plates speeding away from a stationary position directly outside the house. Contacting the local L.A. County Sheriff's Office, they said someone would come out to take a report. While waiting, we conducted our own mini investigation and it was clear to see that the BB could not have been fired from that car because my pickup was parked in the driveway obstructing its pathway. That vehicle was evidently a decoy and lookout covering for someone who had likely fled on foot the opposite direction. I waited there at least two hours to give a report, but nobody came out. This was La Cañada, an upscale community where emergency response times are otherwise minimal. Work was waiting on me; I had a business to run. Delbert later told me sheriff deputies arrived not long after I left. In the process of interviewing him, he said they attempted to convince him that I am some kind of bad guy he should not be associating with. Delbert said, "I've known you a long time, Mark. I know better."

Working as a driver in the motion picture industry is a coveted occupation. Over the years I have seen many people attempt to land that job without success. In a place where nepotism runs rampant, the powers that be like to think they are in control, only permitting union entry to those whom they are approving of. It is for them to determine who is accepted within the ranks of their cabal and it is for them to oust those they are disapproving of. It would be no different for me. In 2001 in a roundabout way, I was served notice of termination regarding my union membership. In my possession I had all the evidence necessary to adequately refute the circumstances and secure my position. A lady named Carol at the union office was appointed as my ambassador and liaison in addressing the matter. Other members described to me how she went to bat for them in time of need, effectively coming through in a pinch. The outstanding issue was not with the union themselves, but with a go-between organization, or so that is what was presented to me. Supposedly, Carol was to be an advocate for members, including me on this occasion. In our telephone conversation, however, she demonstrated no interest in helping me. I pressed the issue, but she informed me there was nothing she could do to assist me. Not satisfied with that, I consulted with at least three attorneys, all of whom informed me I had a clear-cut case they were willing to accept. I called Carol again at the union office and told her I had obtained legal advice that clearly supported my position. I mistakenly believed this would be helpful in us working together to rectify the situation. The only thing she was interested in were the names of those lawyers, demanding to know their identities. This lady was not about to help me and was in no manner of things acting alone. While coming to the rescue of approved fellow members, her distinct objective was to usher me out the door. Carol, as it turned out, was the wife of the man I previously mentioned, Lee. I had become a singled out, unaccommodated subject they were attempting to ouster from their cabal. A few years later I was made abreast of my assigned status: "eligible for reinstatement." There was absolutely no ambiguity to their motives. If I retained legal counsel and pursed the matter, I have no doubt I would have ended up dead. I do not doubt that to this day. I know what these guys are capable of; I know way too much. At the time, I figured that if I just dropped the matter, then they would leave me alone. I still owned and operated Rolling Dumpsters. Even though being a driver in the industry would have prospered me significantly, my business was on track to render me a wealthy man. Very wealthy.

In September of 2002 I moved into a large house at the north end of the San Fernando Valley. A friend had been renting the entire home himself and was sub renting to several roommates. I had lived there for a brief period during 1999 and was looking to move back in, but my guy was on his way out, so he put me in contact with the owner. I was not previously acquainted with this guy, who come to find out had numerous aliases and to this day I still cannot tell you what his real name actually is. Both my friend and the owner were involved in the motion picture industry. My friend is a cordial, likeable guy and was experiencing digestive ailments of an unknown etiology. At the time he was moving out, there was some kind of disagreement between him and that landlord, but he had a far worse conflict with one certain roommate residing there. That dude turned out to be one of the meanest human beings I have ever crossed paths with. What is more, he had a distinct and extreme disdain for my friend. After a few months of living there, I began to suspect my buddy's digestive ailments were no coincidence.

One day when I returned home from work, a large group of people were in the front room speaking with that roommate and the owner. I attempted to make out what was on the papers and photos they were passing around between them as I entered the house and walked by, but could not. Reacting to my presence, there was clearly an uneasiness about them as they attempted to conceal what they had been looking at. The landlord approached me later, demanding residents of the home use a different door to enter and exit making it all the more obvious whatever was being discussed among them that day was something that was being hidden from me.

During my stay there, that wretched roommate began talking about poisons. He sounded like a parrot repeating many of the exact same things I heard from the union guys years earlier and it appeared his knowledge about the subject came as a result of that secretive meeting in the front room that day. It was a topic he suddenly became preoccupied with, constantly discussing it in addition to the subject of child molesters. He spoke about alkaline batteries, spicy foods to adulterate, and even uranium. He mentioned oxalic acid and its potential to disrupt the cellular metabolism of cholesterol, adversely impacting the human body and inducing vascular occlusion. I remembered from my college studies that oxalic acid is present in the Krebs tricarboxylic acid cycle. Pressing questions arose in my mind: How would he know this? Better yet, *why* would he know this? And why did he suddenly embark upon the subject immediately on the heels of that clandestine meeting? It was not too long thereafter that some of the roommates and myself began to discovered the true character of that man.

Nan was one of the few decent people who lived in that house at the time. A friendly lady with slight stature, she was a few years older than me. She warned another roommate, Mike, and I about the evil deeds of our cohabiter, having become aware of him long before we moved in. She told of his legal savvy and nasty things he did to people. According to Nan, the girl who occupied my bedroom just prior to me had been served legal documents naming her as a defendant in a civil case. The official court documents had been stamped with the clerk's seal indicating authenticity. Making an appearance at the date and time required, the girl discovered the case did not exist. Her name was not on the court calendar and they had no evidence of the case otherwise. She had evidently been served some kind of fake documents. Nan said that nasty roommate confessed to have been responsible for producing the paperwork, complete with an official clerk's stamp. At one point he even confessed to me his liability.

One day while traveling on the freeway, I saw Nan driving the opposite direction. When I mentioned it to her later, she said she was coming from the Sheriff's station where she had been a number of times to meet with a detective addressing matters regarding our roommate. Although no criminal charges were filed against him to the best of my knowledge, Nan had valid reasons for complaint. One day I witnessed an event myself that was far beyond just a little bit troubling. This guy is a fairly large man, while Nan petite and was battling cancer. He was standing there, fists clenched and shouted, "I'll kill you, Nan! I'll rip your throat out and drag you across the floor!" I could not believe my eyes and ears. Never before or ever since have I witnessed such an event. It was absolutely horrific. With my jaw agape I looked at Nan, but she exhibited no reaction whatsoever. As she stated it to me later, she simply expected that kind of behavior from that dude; an attestation to the character of a truly rotten human being. Fortunately, that was the extent of his rage that evening.

One day Nan, Mike, and I decided to split the cost of a background check on this fellow. Although we dug up a little dirt, the report did not indicate anything terribly shocking or horrendous. The fact of the matter was, we did not want to live with this guy and addressed our concerns with landlord several times, but he was not willing to hear a word about it. Somewhere along the way we learned our not-so-wonderful roomy prepared legal documents for him, therefore he was an asset not to be parted with. After not receiving any reprieve from the landlord, Mike and I went down to the local L.A.P.D. police station seeking resolve and were given an appointment to meet with a detective. At that meeting the officer showed interest in our explanations, even bringing in a colleague to listen in. Nothing materialized from it, but at least we told what needed to be told.

Mike was a decent fellow to live with. Several years younger than myself, he became like a little bother to me. He also connected well with my children, which I really appreciated. Mike is a good size man, but extremely gentle in character. One day Mike was playing pool with Dennis, another roommate forced upon us despite our repeated objections. The miniature pool table was set up in a common area where Mike and Dennis had played a few times prior. My young children and I watched that day as the game ended with Mike sinking the eight ball. Dennis, a little guy likely weighing under a hundred pounds, held the pool stick inverted and hit Mike with it dropping him to his knees. The blow landed on the side of Mike's neck barely missing his jugular vein and carotid artery. Contrary to the dictates of my conscience and exercising great restraint, I only went so far as to separate Dennis from the pool stick. In immediate compliance, he took a seat exactly where I instructed him to. He went to jail and Mike went to the emergency room.

The following day Mike, Nan, and I were discussing what had taken place. The pool table had been removed; there was to be no more of that. With a tremendous welt on his neck, Mike shared with us about how the medical staff at the hospital informed him the injury could have cost him his life. Had he been struck just a smidgeon off from where the blow landed, that likely would have been it for him. We were nevertheless thankful for the removal of a roommate we had been forced to live with despite our objections. It was not without cost, but Mike was heralded as a hero for making it happen. The new-found calming peace permeating the atmosphere of our home proved to be short-lived though. At that very moment, Dennis came strolling in the door. "What in the world are you doing here?!" I exclaimed. "The jails were overcrowded, so they let me go," said Dennis, a two-strike violent felon the landlord knowingly inserted into our home directly following his paroled release from prison. As we picked our jaws up off the floor, the suspicion among us was that strings must have been pulled somewhere. That other terrible roomy frequently spoke of and wrote in crazy letters to housemates about some connection he and the owner had with a Los Angeles City councilman.

Those suspicions may have been confirmed one morning when I observed the then city councilman, later to become mayor, Antonio Villaraigosa, standing in that same living room alongside a uniformed L.A.P.D. officer. It was early that morning and I heard people talking out in the living room. Stepping outside my bedroom to see what the commotion was, I saw Dennis walking away from the two of them. My initial thought was that our roommate was in some kind of trouble with the law yet again. It had to be him or possibly even one of the other roommates, I figured. The two men made eye contact with me, but nothing was said so I went back to my bedroom wanting nothing to do with whatever trouble whoever was in. When I saw Dennis was still there later, I asked him what was going on. Eluding my question, he jokingly remarked they were there to see me. Seeing that cop for what was likely the first time, it would not be the last. He was the same one who walked into Foothill Division Police Station and re-lieved an officer taking my stolen trailer report. We would also cross paths at Marie Callender's restaurant in Pasadena a few years after that as I chronicle in chapter 10.

Our landlord moved in a number of characters during my time living there. Dennis was a self-professed devil worshipper with a variety of demonic tattoos adorning his skin. His intravenous drug use met eye-to-eye with other individuals our landlord shepherded in, including another certain fellow. When the drug abusing clique residing with us threw a party one day, this other guy presented a little tiny glass bottle containing a liquid substance. Responding to my inquiry, he said, "It's vitamin K." I still had no idea what it was, so he further explained it was ketamine, an animal tranquilizer. He proceeded to dip a cigarette into the open top wetting the end. After allowing it to dry for several minutes, he lit it up and passed it around. I objectively observed as it made its way around the huddled group and was eventually offered to me, but I declined of course, not identifying myself as an animal in need of tranquilization although I may have made such an observation regarding the others. Curious what the effects were, I watched as they seemed to move about like wafting clouds in the sky. It appeared as if floating became their means of locomotion. I was absolutely heart wrenched, though, to observe the long-term impact drugs had on that man's brain. Claiming to have received an inheritance from his grandmother, he spent $15,000 on the installation of the most incredible stereo system I have ever seen in a vehicle. It was installed in his pickup truck which was valued at somewhere around $7,000.

Although I was curious to see how the "vitamin K" affected them, I certainly did not like what I saw that night. A pretty young lady I had never seen before, probably in her early 20s, was an attendee at the get-together. She also took a puff from the cigarette, although I am not sure if she was aware that it had been tainted. Soon thereafter, she too was scooting around on cloud nine. I was concerned for her safety and did not see her leave that evening. The behavior exhibited by the group that night troubled me greatly; there was just an evil feel about it all. Later, as their numbers thinned out, those few remaining moved their activity out to the soundstage near where Dennis's bedroom was located. Their group included another tenant the owner moved in, a woman in her 20s or 30s who resided there only a few months. According to Dennis, she was some kind of sexual bondage prostitute. Another man about my age joined them late in the evening, arriving in a red minitruck. I felt really creeped out when one of them said, "He looks just like you." In my concern for the safety of that one young lady, I inquired about her. Supposedly, the guy in the red minitruck gave her a ride home and to the best of my knowledge she never returned to that big ugly house on the mountainside overlooking the San Fernando Valley.

After so many unpleasant experiences at that house, I could not move out of there fast enough. Before I finally did, the owner had a few more curveballs up his sleeve. He lived nearby and paid us regular visits, always doing so with a confrontational predisposition. A new set of "house rules" showed up regularly and so did the questionable characters we were forced to live with: drug users, party animals, pot heads, and prostitutes. Placing a lock on my bedroom door did not put a stop to intruders. Tools I had locked away in a storage closet disappeared; tools that I had previously declined to lend out when it was asked of me. In the garage was a row of four refrigerators with two or three tenants assigned to each one. Items in them were missing and adulterated nonstop. Putting locks on them proved ineffective also; the shenanigans continued unceasingly. The value of the food items I discarded while living there added up to somewhere in the neighborhood of $3,000. Although to me the cost was significant, it may well have preserved my life.

Not long after I moved out in May of 2004, I was informed Nan had passed away. The news came as a surprise because she was expected to survive and appeared to have much life left in her. I was not the only one that thought her death was premature. To add insult to injury, I was told those devious roommates were pilfering through Nan's belongings the very day she died.

Living in that large house was a bad experience indeed. Although it did not occur to me at the time, I believe what happened there was a setup. Many of my belongings were stolen during my stay. The filing cabinet and business records in my bedroom office had been rummaged through a number of times. Cash, tools, and receipts were filched. An astonishing array of characters were purposefully brought in so I would have to live with them. It was the place where I got my first dose of a toxic substance. I just could not get out of there fast enough. During my stay there, one of the roommates came up with a very fitting name for that big ol' ugly house: The Mausoleum.

When I moved out of the Mausoleum in May of 2004, I had not been feeling well. I was only 37 years of age and had been in good health, yet was feeling very lethargic. That continued for the next several months. The holiday season was approaching and I was looking forward to the slow down during that time which is typical of Hollywood. My business had really taken off and I was working an overabundance of hours. I determined I was going to seize the opportunity and see a doctor to figure out why I had been feeling so yucky. Just before the holiday break arrived though, I found myself being pried off my bathroom floor and loaded onto a paramedic's gurney. Sudden and severe pains wrenched my gut and I was found to have an exceedingly high fever. I was admitted to the hospital and kept a few days during which time the doctors thought they had identified the cause. In reality, what was diagnosed as the cause was rather a symptom of what actually occurred. My symptoms and experience matched categorically precise with what those union thugs described to me several years prior. Just as they had said, the floodgates were opened for unabated diabolical persecution. I returned to work immediately after being discharged from my hospital stay. Afterall, I had a business to operate. Within a matter of days, one of the location managers using Rolling Dumpsters, a certain man I had become untrusting of, stated to me virtually verbatim my entire experience. It was quite odd because I had not informed this fellow nor any of his colleagues about the nature of my circumstances. Not only did I find it odd, but also very troubling because it seemed as if he was mocking me in the process. After yet another adverse experience working with him, I finally told the man I had too many problems on his shows and would no longer be accepting orders from him. His response was, "I'll make sure to tell all my friends."

In the early 1950s the Central Intelligence Agency began covert illegal experiments on American citizens wherein they manipulated their minds and mental functioning. Operating under the code name

MK-Ultra, their unaware victims were subjected to torture, hypnosis, and a wide variety of mind-altering drugs. Other institutions became involved in the activity including the F.B.I., N.S.A., I.R.S., hospitals, universities, prisons, and large corporations. The clandestine exploits continued on into the mid-1970s, but not before many people lost cognitive abilities or even their lives. Several of their targets committed suicide. MK-Ultra was spotted on the radar in 1975 by a U.S. Senate committee investigating abuses by the four government agencies I noted above. When a congressional probe was initiated, the C.I.A. director made a valiant effort to obstruct the investigation. He succeeded in overseeing the destruction of nearly all documentation. Tens, if not hundreds of millions of U.S. taxpayer dollars were spent on the project. When Sirhan Sirhan was brought to justice for the assassination of Robert F. Kennedy, his attorney claimed he had been "Operating under MK-Ultra mind control techniques."

When the unfortunate news stories involving rampage murders are broadcast on media outlets, we have often heard the assailant claim they were operating under the control of some other force at work within their mind. Oftentimes, they have made seemingly wild claims about government agencies reading their minds and thoughts. Could it be MK-Ultra never did cease? Perhaps it was resurrected? Demonic activity is certainly a viable candidacy to assign blame to. The most frequent culprit people identify appears to be mental illness, but could not all these things be working in conjunction? I think so. I also think that it is important for us to understand that all of it involves terrible evils which can ultimately be traced back to Satan himself.

As I bring this subject up regarding our historical stain MK-Ultra, I want to point out a few things we should all be aware of. Consider the time period when these events occurred. Technology was lagging far behind where it stands today. Advancements in today's technology facilitates a greater ability to achieve the objectives of MK-Ultra, does it not? Do not begin to think for even one minute that wayward individuals would refrain from employing such technology in like manner now. Those claims from rampaging murderers have been repeated so many times, it cannot be merely coincidence. Although they are promptly dismissed as deranged crazed individuals suffering from mental health issues, and likely many are, remember what happens to targeted persons: "They end up dead, in jail, or move far away. They go crazy and appear to be mentally ill." It just fits the narrative. Hearing those claims repeated quite a few times over, I believe that same surreptitious agenda is alive and active today.

Certain people working in those same government agencies today have become quite polarized, possessing objectives such as disarming the American population. If enough mass shootings occur, then perhaps they could convince everybody that government need needs to confiscate all firearms. Motive after motive for what they are doing can be identified, but will the perpetrators of the diabolical agenda lay down their own weapons of warfare? It did not happen when they were discovered in 1975 and they are not about to suddenly become penitent and admit their wrongdoing now. It will take the American people identifying what is flying under the radar and rising up against it once again. I may be labeled as the crazy one for suggesting such things, but I do not care. I do not care what they think or say about me, there is a message that must be told; please hear what I am telling you. The people I have discussed within the pages of this book are wielding that same weapon again today, yet thoroughly updated with modern technology. The modern-day equivalent of MK-Ultra is being utilized indiscriminately against the American people. Used responsibly, this could have been a valuable crime-fighting tool, especially in consideration of terrorism. That is not the case, however, because countless unwitting American citizens are being driven crazy and there is a trail of dead bodies lying in the wake. We cannot stand for this any longer. The cloak of darkness must be cast off and these evils must be exposed.

Working in the motion picture industry is a lucrative career for many people, especially in Southern California. The majority of them typically hold personal values which are markedly different than mine. In no manner of thinking do I consider myself better than them because of this or for any other reason. A beautiful thing contained within the freedoms we enjoy as Americans is that we have the freedom to make our own personal decisions. For example, we may choose to accept Jesus Christ as our Lord and Savior or we may choose to reject doing so. That is in fact, a God-given freedom. What is important to understand, however, is that as outlined in the Constitution of the United States, our freedoms come from our Creator and not from government nor any other entity. If one fallaciously believes that government provides our freedoms, then be advised loved one, government can take those freedoms away. The fact of the matter is that, as we have been endowed by our Creator with certain unalienable rights, governments are instituted among man to secure these rights.

As for Christians, we are given a directive to love everyone, even our enemies. This is a tall order if you ask me. It is something counterintuitive to human reasoning. Those outside of the Church could certainly benefit from following such a directive as well. Of course, I can share with you from my personal experience that this can only occur with any measure of sincerity via tapping into God's love. It seems impossible to love a person who is persecuting or harming us in some way, but with the love of God living in us, it is something we can and should do. In the process of it all, perhaps the perpetrator may be impacted by the love of God displayed in us and choose to give their heart to Jesus Christ. As only those who have personally experienced it can testify, His love changes everything, including us from the inside out.

Among the multitude of individuals employed in the entertainment industry there exists a wide variety of talent. I once watched a man auditioning for an on-screen role. After he was given a script to read from, he pretty much memorized its several paragraphs having read it only once through. He recited the lines with precision, never referring back to the script. I watched a couple more auditions that day and those people read directly from the script even after previewing it. I remarked about that man's photographic memory to the casting people who told me it is not uncommon among professional actors. I have seen incredible talents demonstrated as cameras rolled. Actors take on the persona of the character portrayed at the literal snap of a finger. Some possess the ability to be moved to tears or even sob uncontrollably at the moment a director calls out, "Rolling!"

Amazing abilities are not limited to those in front of the cameras. Film sets are designed and constructed by those who execute their occupations with significant talent and abilities of their own. Scenic artists, being no commonplace house painters, apply their trade doing such things as making something brand new take on the appearance of something old, tattered, and worn out. Set dressers, with a surprising eye for detail, come in like movers and make a set come alive. On and on it goes from directors, to lighting, to post-production sound effects and editing – amazing talents are demonstrated by countless gifted individuals.

All the while, most of these wonderfully talented people profess an unswerving loyalty to their respective unions wherein they have attained the distinct status of having put on their shoes. My question is, would all these gifted people retain this loyalty if they were afforded insider knowledge regarding the dynamics of wayward union leadership and the corrupt nature of the political persons and causes they support? The fact is, some are aware, but just how many and how much do they really know? I believe the majority possess limited awareness, but since their union takes good care of them, their loyalties are sustained. They enjoy wonderful employment benefits, therefore their union allegiance remains unswervingly devout. Membership is pretty much required to maintain devotion to union leadership and causes irrespective of that leadership's dignity or deviance. In all reality, most would be fearful of speaking out against wrongs in such places because doing so would adversely implicate themselves. Conversely, there are those in the inner group who are very much aware of these workings, operating as cogs in the gearworks. There are a select few who are not at all aware of the union forces at work. This group undoubtedly comprises the fewest in number and are inclined to hold the viewpoint that whatever their union and its leadership does is dignified, acting only upon the beneficial interests of the constituency. This person likely lacks the experience of the former groups I mentioned. Allocated sufficient time and opportunity, they too will eventually be indoctrinated, at least to some extent.

Exhibiting the aptitude the hardworking people of the industry do, I hold the opinion that a respectable percentage, in all likelihood most, ultimately want what is fair, right, and good. However, apostacy equates to danger for them. If a few began to speak up, then perhaps that might spur a movement. Then the smoke and mirrors of diabolical deception can and will be put to flight. My prayer for so many years has been and continues to be that God would cast off that cloak of darkness, shine His light in revealing the truth, and allow all people to see these things for what they truly are. No more lies. No more deception. I pray God would allow us to hold accountable here in this world those who are responsible for executing Satan's objectives. If the proper individuals are exposed, criminally prosecuted, and subsequently incarcerated, then that would serve at least two important benefits. Firstly, society at large would be protected from dangerous people who pose a threat, which is why we lock up criminals in the first place. Secondly, they would be in a place wherein they could contemplate their misdeeds and be afforded an opportunity to sincerely repent before our Creator. In doing so, one would be avoiding a day of judgement far more severe than the one that got them admitted to the gray bar hotel. This has been my earnest prayer for a very long time. Perhaps it is yours as well? If so, it is time for you too to take a stand against corruption and evil. Satan's objectives are to steal, kill, and, destroy. The guilty parties have been his instruments of wickedness for a long time – long before I appeared on their radar as a target. They are slaughtering innocent people and Christians are the bull's-eye object. Dear friend, regardless of what your sincerely held spiritual beliefs are, regardless of where you stand in regard to political loyalties, union pledges or personal ties, it is time for you to come out from among them and take a stand for what is right and good. Evil must be defeated. Our nation as we know it lies in the balance. More importantly, the ultimate fate of human souls are at stake. What is of great importance and what weighs so heavily upon my heart is that you, reading this now, consecrate your own heart to Jesus Christ. If you have not done so, I invite you to do that right here, right now. Just take a moment to speak with Him. No ostentatious oration is required for any person's prayer to be heard by God. In fact, just the opposite holds true. Simply speak and speak simply to the One who created you and tell Him that you are giving your heart to Him. At the conclusion of this book I will offer this invitation once again and provide a few more important details.

If and when you face such persecution (I pray you never do), a proper response by a child of God can prove to be extremely challenging. The Biblical directive to rejoice in suffering is counterintuitive to human reasoning. Our carnal nature possesses a propensity to respond with bellicose retortion, revealing within ourselves that we have plenty of room for spiritual growth. Loving a person who maltreats us is something Christians who experience it must learn to do. It becomes a choice. This is a privilege loved ones, and affords us opportunity to grow spiritually in deep ways. Becoming imbittered, although not the right reaction, is not abnormal. Scripture instructs us to rid ourselves of bitterness, but how can we do that especially when subjected to torment and tyranny? That is a tall order and one I have been forced to wrestle with for a long time, yet still have room for improvement. I can offer you the best suggestion I know which is based upon my own experience: Ask God to help you. Ask him to replace that bitterness with His love. The unconditional, incredible, and downright unreasonable love of our Creator working in us and through us can and will come in like a flood. It overwhelmingly displaces bitterness, hatred, and anger in such a way that is humanly impossible. His love changes everything, inclusive of broken humanity and does so from the inside out. It equips us to go well beyond our own abilities, far beyond the expulsion of bitterness to a place where we can even love those who persecute us. The love of God finds life and purpose all the way to the place of severe torture and martyrdom.

The Bible says when the power of darkness comes in, God will come like a pent-up flood, lifting up a standard against it (Isaiah 59:19). The Lord our God will put the enemy to flight. This is the Living Word of the Living God. His Word is true. The enemies of God will be met with the irresistible power of His Spirit. Just where is His Spirit? He is at work in the lives of the redeemed. At the moment a person receives Jesus Christ as Lord and Savior, they are marked as His own, receiving the indwelling presence of the One who made them. If we call upon and afford Him the opportunity, the Holy Spirit of God, working in and through the Body of Christ, can and will extinguish the flames of hell around us today. When the power of darkness comes in, the power of darkness must go! Be advised dear friend, that knowing Christ not only means sharing in the power of His Resurrection, but it also includes sharing in His sufferings.

CHAPTER 10

PARTICIPATING IN THE SUFFERINGS OF CHRIST

I want to know Christ – yes, to know the power of his resurrection
and participation in his sufferings, becoming like him in his death,
and so, somehow, attaining to the resurrection from the dead.

Philippians 3:10-11

Now if we are children, then we are heirs –
heirs of God and co-heirs with Christ, if indeed
we share in his sufferings in order that we
may also share in his glory.

Romans 8:17

IN A SUBCONSCIOUS quest to make others more approving or loving of us, it is a natural human inclination to portray ourselves more highly than we really ought to. We may conceal our faults while magnifying the better aspects of our personhood. It is my desire to completely cut through any narcissistic pretentions. In no way do I intend to deceive myself or my readers. I am no angel; I am far from perfect. I possess no self-delusion of being without faults or liabilities. Much to my chagrin, I have done some really stupid things in my lifetime resulting in terrible regret. At times I have faced suffering as a rightful consequence of wrongdoings I committed. I have also endured suffering, and a large measure of it, because I bear the Name of Jesus Christ, which is a true privilege. It was God who called me to ministry and minister His Gospel I will. If you want a goody-two-shoes preacher with a perfect past, then I am not your guy. I have been called from my mother's womb; to be disobedient to that call would not result well for me. Enduring the hardships I have and revealing the evils involved is the primary calling upon my life. Along the way there have been many times I have cried out to God telling Him I want no part of it. These adversities, which I continue to experience, are not all about me. This is the very reason I have written this book.

In this chapter I share stories from many of the challenges I have faced. These are just a select few albeit some of the most extreme. I have arranged them in chronological order for the most part, although I do jump around a little for the sake of clarity and continuity. Dates are provided along the way to assist in achieving this objective and to help place the entirety of it all in proper context.

Recall from chapter eight wherein I discussed potential lawsuits, whistleblowers, and targeted persons. Regarding that, allow me to ask you the following questions: What if one of those potential whistleblower/subject settlements took place and, unbeknownst to the perpetrators, the subject already had knowledge of their operational procedures? Let's say the union and/or their cohorts discover this after the fact, having already agreed to a clandestine settlement with the whistleblower. They have initiated the process and then come to find out the targeted subject has already been indoctrinated to their ways. He obviously knows too much! How then would they proceed? What kind of harassments, poisonings, and evils would that unfortunate person be subjected to? What do they do to such a person? Perhaps one may only begin to consider the possibilities, but this is exactly what has been happening with me. The architects of that diabolical agenda scheme and plan things most people could never conjure up on their own. I know that if I schemed and plotted my whole life through, I could never dream up anything nearly as harmful to a human being as are the things they have done and continue to do to me. Their weapons of warfare inflict deep wounds. Until the weapon is removed a wound cannot begin to heal. The inner person is lacerated and a festering infection persists. The injury only grows, bearing etiological responsibility for the resulting systemic sepsis of the human character. The victim would much rather die than survive even one minute longer living subjected to such evils. It takes terribly deviant minds to produce the tactics and strategies they do. It takes a connection to the ultimate source of that agenda: Satan himself. For me, there is absolutely no reason I should still be alive in this world. It has required my unswerving attention focused upon Jesus Christ to sustain me. That is why He gave me those dreams I described at the very beginning of chapter one.

My Uncle Jim was one of the best men I ever knew. He was kind hearted and fiercely loyal to family. He and Aunt Doris did not have children of their own, so as his younger brother's son, I was like a son to him. Jim was well aware of the challenges I had been facing and was more than willing to lend me a hand in any way he could. When Rolling Dumpsters started to grow, so did the need of additional help. Uncle Jim started to drive for the business and would have undoubtedly become an integral part of it had his life not been cut short in August of 2002.

The mother of my children and I regularly met in Pomona, our designated location for the weekend exchange. I was quite surprised one Friday afternoon in August of 2002 when Uncle Jim came driving through the Carl's Jr. parking lot where I had been waiting for my children to arrive. We were 40 miles away from home and it was highly unusual for him to just happen to be there. As I was waving to him, he almost drove right past me. Thinking that he did not see me, I nearly jumped in front of his car to flag him down. He appeared very reluctant when he stopped and then acted as if he did not even have the time of day for me. That was extremely uncharacteristic of Uncle

Jim. Never before did he act in such a way and I was left baffled by his behavior as he promptly departed.

Shortly thereafter my children arrived with their mother. Usually we headed back to my home right away, but this time they said they were hungry and wanted something at Carl's Jr. Their mother went on her way and I took them in to grab a bite to eat. Entering the door, I looked back at my pickup truck and took notice of a young man in a small AAA service truck pulling into the parking lot. He paused, looked around, then drove right over next to my truck. The parking lot and the restaurant were unusually crowded that afternoon. I had always parked near the entrance, but was unable to this time. I left my vehicle positioned across the lot in a place that was not visible from inside. I had an alarm and the truck locked, so I did not perceive any kind of threat. After eating, we made the drive back, stopping for fuel near my home. While the pump was fueling us up, I opened the back door and took out the light jacket I had with me. Putting it on, I placed my hands in the pockets and felt what I thought was a receipt. In the process of running a business I kept receipts for every purchase I made and figured this was one I had simply left behind. When I pulled it out and saw what it was, I was shocked. I was holding a little tiny zip-lock baggie containing a white powder. From the filling station I drove straight to the local sheriff's station and explained what happened. They took the baggie, wrote up a report indicating narcotics were found and that was the last I ever heard about it. How it got there, I cannot tell you beyond conjecture. To this day I am convinced it was a drug planted on me that I was supposed to get caught with. The divorce and custody battles were ongoing at that time, so I considered that my children's mother may have been involved, especially since it happened when our children were with me. On the other hand, those union boys had been pursuing me mercilessly. Could they have been responsible for all this? I replayed the events over and over in my mind. Why was the parking lot and restaurant so abnormally crowded? What was the strange occurrence with that AAA service vehicle all about? When he pulled in, he looked around the lot, appeared to spot my truck, then drove up and parked right next to it. What about Uncle Jim? That was downright bizarre. Was he somehow aware somebody was targeting me at that time and was looking out for my safety? It seems I was not supposed to notice him that day. Did the perpetrators spot Jim and I in our brief exchange? I think he and I were seen greeting one another by the guilty parties. That was the last time I saw Uncle Jim alive. He died unexpectedly just a few days later of a sudden heart attack. He was 64.

My dad and I were left perplexed by our loss. I told him everything that happened that day and nothing seemed right about it to either of us. We had more questions than answers as we were both simply unaccepting that Jim's passing happened in the natural course of events. As the months and years have passed, I have become more and more convinced that my uncle was murdered.

Just over a year later, the pastor of the church I was attending passed away suddenly and unexpectedly at just 49 years of age. He had just led a prayer service and was exiting the platform when he collapsed, dying in the hospital two days later. The cause of death was said to be hemorrhage from a brain aneurism. At the time it appeared to be simply an unfortunate event, but as time went by, I became more suspicious. He had previously said a few things which led me to believe he had knowledge of the circumstances I had been enduring. The fact he was a pastor made him a target according to my informed indoctrination in the motion picture industry. He was not only the pastor of a large congregation, but was *my* pastor. If there were not so many others, then I would certainly be dismissive at any suggestion of wrongdoing.

During the time I resided at the Mausoleum, I frequently traveled a route that took me from the eastbound 118 Freeway to the southbound 5 Freeway. In the process of all the harassment it was becoming more than simply evident I was being targeted on the roadways and this was the place they chose to target me. Navigating any large city entails a measure of challenges with other motorists and Southern California certainly epitomizes that reality. A fair share of things will happen on the road, but with nearly two million miles of driving experience, I am no novice. That transition from the 118 to the 5 became the site of an unreasonable number of incidents. Usually I was alone, but on one occasion there were witnesses. My older sister and all our children were in the truck with me when a minitruck displaying foreign license plates made an abrupt move across several lanes nearly colliding with us. Having encountered this exact same thing on numerous occasions over a short period of time at the same place, it was obvious the reckless maneuver was intentional. Sure, it happens all the time that someone makes a last-second decision when they are about to miss their turn, but it was happening on purpose. The single occupant, a middle-aged male driver, was snickering. We followed behind the guy while speaking with a 911 operator who exhibited nothing but disinterest in the call.

Then along came another man a short time later. Driving alone in an older white van, he did the exact same thing in the exact same place, this time rubbing the passenger side of his vehicle against the fender of the trailer I was towing. The two of us pulled off onto the right shoulder of the freeway where he was apologetic. Resulting black marks were visible on the sliding door of his van, although minimal. He checked right then and there, opening and closing that door freely without any difficulty. The fender on my Rolling Dumpster ended up with some of his white paint on it, but was otherwise undamaged. Mutually agreeing to leave the matter at that, we parted ways exchanging no information. Leave it at that however, he did not. The entire incident was, as I later came to realize, a set-up from the start. Several months later I was served a legal notice informing me that a court judgement had been entered against me. Upon investigation, I learned that it stemmed from that fender non-bender with this man, Julio. He submitted a claim with his insurance company naming me as the responsible party. The insurance company referred the claim to an underhanded, aggressive collection agency that somehow was awarded judgment without my knowledge. As soon as I discovered what was going on, I filed for a court hearing myself. At the hearing I fully expected the matter to be properly rectified and that at the very least I would be provided opportunity to rightly give sworn testimony regarding the truth of what actually occurred. That, however, was not to be. I was absolutely shocked when the judge stated he was unwilling to set aside the judgement entered against me. Recalling what those union guys said so many years prior, I figured the case had been steered along pathways comprised of their constituents. This was entirely a set-up, from start to finish. They were coming after me and my business. I suppose that I could have pursed the matter in appellate court, but the time and expense involved was in no way worth it to me. I could produce way more income in the time it would require to contest the case. Fearing they intended to seize my business assets, I paid the $4,200 judgment. I later returned to that 118 East to 5 South transition road in an attempt to identify what it was about this particular stretch of freeway that qualified its use in such a way. The prerequisite became distinctly evident when I observed the placement of freeway cameras. On the 118 leading up to the transition and on the transition itself, there were no cameras. Travel a short distance on the 5 afterwards and cameras are installed. From that observation I deduced the intent was to provoke me to be caught on camera retaliating against another motorist who had performed a dangerously stupid, yet obviously intentional cut-off in the area immediately preceding which had no cameras.

All the while I continued to be harassed in just about every possible way. I had acquired enough savings to make a down payment toward the purchase of a home, but I was focused on expanding my business. My financial resources would have been consumed by a mortgage leaving less for the growth of Rolling Dumpsters. Moving out of the Mausoleum in May of 2004, I rented a small two-bedroom home in Tujunga. Upon returning there from work I found various items around the house were not exactly as I had left them. Somebody was entering my home when I was not there. Unlike the Mausoleum, however, nothing was missing, at least not that I noticed. Before long, my neighbors there began exhibiting clues someone had gotten to them, even those I had befriended. Oddball occurrences at home after home evolved into status quo.

When I moved from the Mausoleum, I had been experiencing a persistent yucky feeling. Six months later in November of 2004, I suddenly became very ill and was hauled off to the hospital in an ambulance. That was just the first of several such experiences I would eventually encounter. Although it was quite severe, it was not as extreme as the poisonings inflicted upon me in the years following. The discharge orders I received after that first hospitalization were echoed in follow-up visits to doctor's offices: do not eat this, do not eat that. By all means, it would be foolish of me to flippantly disregard professional medical advice, but I knew that what they identified was merely a symptom and not the actual cause. I adhered unswervingly to their advice. My diet changed drastically, but I continued to experience the symptoms for quite some time, shedding about 65 pounds of weight. My countenance was gaunt and frail. I was feeling every bit the same on the inside as what my exterior showed, if not worse. Consuming a puree diet of high-quality foods and avoiding repeat incidences of toxic exposure eventually facilitated the return of my health. None of these approaches can hold the same effectiveness as praying to the King of kings though. I diligently pressed in, petitioning my Lord for the provision of His healing touch. Once I recovered, I was determined to demonstrate that what I had experienced was an acute traumatic gastrointestinal injury. I then consumed almost nothing but the foods items I had been advised to avoid. I ate as much as I could, purposefully attempting to induce a repeat occurrence of what I had previously experienced. After several months it became obvious the condition diagnosed was merely a symptom separate of the actual cause. A few years later I repeated the same experiment with gluten products which produced the same results; I was not suffering from a gluten intolerance either.

It had been suggested to me at some point that perhaps I had been consuming something in my regular diet which I had an allergy or aversion to. At that point I created a plan to identify any such food product. I began with a multi-day, water-only fast after which time I reintroduced food items back into my diet only one at a time, waiting approximately three days before including the addition of another. During the first few days of consuming nothing but blueberries, I expected to see something colorfully blue as an end result. Much to my amazement, what came out was actually green. I paid particularly close attention to highly allergenic foods. Peanuts, strawberries, shellfish, and dairy were among those. I continued the modified diet over a period of several months and it involved a wide variety of food products. Attempts to isolate and identify a malefactor proved elusive; none were found. I legitimately ruled out dietary intake as the etiology of the affliction. I knew the real cause of what I had been experiencing. I also understood why any person or doctor would suggest alternative causes. After all, if any person told me what I had been telling them, then I would question their mental health. In all likelihood, I would suggest an alternate cause and that is exactly what was being proposed to me. I heeded their advice nevertheless, but that did not keep me from pursuing actions which would ultimately prove or disprove causative origins.

One day my children and I decided to order take-out pizza for dinner. After placing the order by telephone, we drove over and picked it up. Inside the restaurant was a man who appeared very familiar to me, but I could not remember who he was or where I had seen him before. When my daughter and I became sick a few hours after dinner, I replayed the events in my mind, finally coming to an exacting realization of where I had seen that man before. He was part of the large group who was speaking with that horrid housemate and the owner when I came home to the Mausoleum that day. He also appeared at Burbank Kawasaki a few weeks later at the same time I was encountering difficulties with a less than affable service manager there. A year or two after that I saw him at a sandwich shop once again. To say the least, I was reluctant to consume that sandwich I had purchased. After eating a few bites of the sandwich I threw it away. Later that day a yucky feeling came over me that persisted for several weeks before finally diminishing. I realized that this fellow is a dangerous man; he is one of them. To the best of my knowledge I have not crossed paths with him since.

The intrusions into my home continued. On many occasions upon returning, I could see someone had been inside. In 2005 I bought a video camera. I set it up every time I left, but for a several weeks nothing happened. Then one day I returned and immediately noticed it was slightly out of place from where I had positioned it. I thought for sure I finally caught somebody. When I tried to play back what I thought was recorded, it was not working. When I attempted to operate it, the zoom was stuck on. The video camera that cost me a few hundred dollars had been sabotaged inside my own locked home. Papers and various items around my home continued to be moved around while I was away. In May of 2005, six months after my first hospitalization, I suddenly fell violently ill again. My suggestions to the emergency room staff regarding the probable cause were only met with condescension. I firmly believe this time around it was from eating food tainted inside my own home. There was certainly ample opportunity and it was unmistakably clear intruders had repeatedly entered during my absence. I was beginning to speak up anyway in spite of whether people believed me or not. Sure they thought I was crazy; I understand how anybody would think that. I was learning to stand up against those evils nevertheless, becoming vocal about it and increasingly bold.

In October of 2006 my dear friend Delbert died. He was the one who had lent me money to start the business. I lived with him and his wife from sometime in 2000 to September of 2002. For reasons unknown to me at the time, he was very concerned about my safety when I moved out. Sometime between 2001 and 2003 he began making claims he was being poisoned. At first, I did not realize any connection. Del repeated it to me a number of times and I responded by asking who would want to poison him. All he would say is, "They want the old man dead." It was when I became mysteriously sickened in 2004 that I began to make the connection. I suspect he discovered somebody messing with my equipment while I had been living with him, somehow catching them in the act and subsequently accepted a settlement offer. He therefore became a whistleblower, just as the union guys described to me some years prior. I directly questioned him regarding the subject, but he hemmed and hawed, clearly avoiding my questions on each and every occasion. As time passed, my suspicions grew and I pressed harder with Del. Only three times did he provide any kind of clue. Firstly, he asked one day, "How much money do you need?" with an emphasis on "much." To me, this was indicative of the generous settlement offer the unions were said to make in such situations. All the money would inevitably make its way back to their own people anyway once they got their politician to seize the assets. Secondly, Delbert said to me, "Mark, I'm afraid I've caused you a lot of problems." He adamantly refused to further elaborate even though I demanded to know specifically what he meant by that statement. Lastly, when I moved out, Del and his wife brought in a live-in caregiver. Many oddball things began to happen and I suspected they got to her. Addressing that very subject I said to him, "I think those guys who've been messing with me got to her." Delbert replied, "I do too. We just have to prove it." At that moment she approached us. Although she was not privy to our conversation, that was the end of that discussion. During her employment expensive belongings increasingly disappeared from Del and Norma's home in addition to the countless other mischiefs that occurred.

Delbert was an easy target at his advanced age. Whatever would ultimately take his life could be easily refuted by anyone accused of nefariously adulterating something he ingested. He knew he was being poisoned, but was unable to take enough preventative measures to adequately protect himself. With exacting precision, the circumstances fit the narrative like a puzzle piece. It all culminated with Del traveling to his home state of Missouri in October of 2006. In chapter eight I shared with you how a targeted person or whistleblower is considered vulnerable when traveling. This proved true for Delbert and again for me in 2021. Experiencing a stroke while in Missouri, my dear friend was returned home on a privately chartered medical flight said to have cost thirty-something thousand dollars. Within a matter of days my best friend was gone. The whistleblower was dead along with his secrets – he took them to the grave never coming out with the truth.

Approximately two months after Del passed, Christian Life Church caught fire reducing the entire sanctuary, fellowship hall, kitchen, and several offices to a heap of ash. Del and Norma had already been at that church in La Crescenta many years by the time I arrived in 1986. We met there and attended together for 20 years. No cause for the conflagration was ever pinpointed. A forensics team searched the following day using dogs specially trained to identify accelerants, but none were found. The recovery process was quite challenging to state it mildly, as the City of Glendale was not exactly accommodating in the rebuilding efforts. I would have otherwise been under the assumption that any local government would exhibit sorrow for such a loss in their community, offering assistance in any way they could. That was not to be as Pastor Tim was advised by someone at the city to demolish the remains as quickly as possible. Following their advice, a demo crew was hired and the remains were carted away in roll-off dumpsters. We came to find out afterwards that if we could have tied into at least one wall that was still standing, then we could have rebuilt everything exactly as it had previously stood. According to an L.A. City engineer and a building inspector who were both personally connected with the church, there were two or three walls that met that definition. It was too late, however, because all those walls were buried in a landfill. Anything built would now be required to meet current guidelines. Everything else on the property was required to be updated as well. All these things were far too costly for the small congregation which was underinsured for the loss as it was. The seating capacity of the new sanctuary was to be determined in direct correlation to the parking spaces available for vehicles resulting in a significant reduction in the building's size. We were not permitted to reconstruct a separate fellowship hall as we had before and the number of offices allowed were far fewer. Those familiar words, "We take down churches," repeat over and over in my mind to this day.

The church eventually hired Terry, an architect who specializes in churches. After drafting plans to submit to the city, he and Pastor Tim arranged a meeting with a man in their building department. Arriving to meet with him as scheduled, they encountered the fellow preoccupied on his cellphone for what was described as an extended period of time. When he finally got off the phone, Tim greeted the fellow and introduced the two of them. In response the man was reported to have said, "You will never see a church built on that piece of property!" Extending his phone to Tim he continued, "Here, call someone who cares!" Tim and Terry were absolutely astonished at what this man said and they looked at each other wondering where that came from. They had never before met with him let alone had any disagreements or falling out. There was constant friction coming from the city of Glendale throughout the ensuing 9 years it took to rebuild the church. Pastor Tim is a kind, gentle, and humble man. He vacated his position in 2010, leaving the project to another man who had previous experience building churches as a pastor. Navigating unnecessary hurdles, the reconstruction project ultimately produced something substantially less than what had previously stood on the property.

Those two events, Delbert's departure and the church fire, occurred within a few short weeks of each other. Another problematic discovery also took place within a timeframe of about six months. My first toxicological analysis revealed the presence of uranium. That was the first of what would eventually be many times the radioactive element was discovered in my body tissues.

Less than two years after our church burned, Sarah Palin's church was firebombed. The arsonist caused extensive damage to that building in Wasilla Alaska, which happens to be the same Christian denomination as the church in La Crescenta California. The former republican governor of Alaska and 2008 vice presidential candidate apologized for the possibility undeserved negative attention had been brought on as a result of her political involvements. The emerging pattern should begin to become evident to our populace at large. I know it has been clear for a select few discerning members within the Body of Christ for quite some time now. Satan and his sycophants do not like churches. They do not like Christians. That old split-hoofed fool has been attempting to destroy the things most precious to God from before man's creation. In America we have been relatively exempt from persecution, but be advised friends, it is happening here. The battle is well under way.

As I mentioned in chapter eight, I was informed that when messing with targeted individuals, they will get to the people around them. One's own family members will accept bribes, especially when it is a generous offer. Wealthy and powerful individuals seek to control people with their wealth; it is all fun and games to them. Although such things are well beyond the means of most of us, they can afford to do it. Remember, "Everyone has their price. Some just cost more than others." Enticed by a fistful of dollars, they will literally stumble over their own loved one's dead body or throw them under a bus because they find the almighty dollar more alluring than the value of the relationship. Many have been persuaded to turn or come against me in a variety of ways. If it were somebody I did not know well, then I might begin to understand, but family members? It happens! Be warned loved ones!

Along the way circumstances revealed the relationship between my younger sister and I became compromised. A mother with three young children can find certain things challenging. Demands on time and attention leave little margin to engage in gainful employment. So it was with my younger sister. For her, a potential job would need to accommodate a schedule in constant flux. That is why my dad thought it would be a good idea for me to put her to work. I was opposed to Dad's proposal from the start. She had been something of a troublemaker, causing serious problems in the family throughout her life. Illogically vindictive, I found myself on the receiving end of her *I'll show you!* approach innumerable times. Against my better judgement, my dad convinced me to employ her. She had no experi-ence driving a large truck, so to get started we spent some time on that. After a couple weeks of training I got her to where she could not only drive the truck, but back up a trailer fairly well too. We made some trailer deliveries and pick-ups together before I finally sent her out on her own.

It did not take long for the union boys to get to her. She had only been working with me a short time when I sent her down to the South Bay area of Los Angeles to make a delivery. What should have taken no more than 3 hours even in heavy traffic turned into an all-day af-fair. I was later informed regarding the nature of the delay. When she was making the delivery, the drivers took notice and invited her to stay for lunch. She willingly obliged, later informing me herself, "But you don't have to pay me for that time." She spoke highly of a group of men I had warned her to avoid. I heard from some of them too. "Your sister is pretty cute," and "She's good for you," were among the comments. My sister's demeanor completely changed after spending a little time with those guys.

One day I walked in on a conversation she was having with our father. Based upon her reaction, I was not supposed to hear what I did after innocently walking up behind her. "What are we supposed to do, make a special tax just for him?!" she exclaimed. My dad was facing her and peered over her shoulder at me as I approached. Whipping around and seeing me, she cast a repugnant glare, obviously disqui-eted by the possibility I heard something she said. That was the extent of what I heard from a conversation that involved me as the subject being discussed. I processed that tidbit over some period of time, eventually concluding it had something to do with my dear friend Delbert, the deceased whistleblower. It just fit the narrative.

My younger sister's tomfooleries did not even begin to end there. We kept one of the company's trucks at her house so that it would be convenient and readily accessible for her. The standing agreement was that it was not to be used for personal matters; she had her own vehicle such things. I allowed this out of a heart of compassion to accommodate her needs. After a short lull in work, a call came in for a delivery. I attempted to make contact, but was unable to reach her. I was by all means perfectly capable of addressing the matter myself, but was committed to keeping my sister busy. What is more, the truck I had with me required repairs which needed to be made before continuing to drive it and I was in the process of making arrangements to send it to a mechanic at the time the order was received. Since I was not able to make contact with my sister, I drove it over to her house anyway thinking I could at least jump in the other truck and get to work. Arriving at her home, she was not there and neither was my other truck. She did not answer any of my repeated attempts to call her, but I was able to make the delivery with the sputtering truck nonetheless. Exasperated, I called our dad who revealed to me what was going on with my wayward sister. It turned out she was on multiday vacation at Disneyland with her children. Without hesitation, she absconded the company truck sans permission or notification. She returned a few days later and it took me yet another few after that to recover the truck. I came to learn she had been using it all along as her personal transportation. I probably should not have placed the trust in her that I did, but from that point on she was going to have to pick up and drop off the truck elsewhere, before and after each workday. That was not to be, however, as she refused to speak with me afterwards even though Rolling Dumpsters became busy again.

Not long thereafter I received notification in the mail from the California Employment Development Department informing me that my employee filed to receive unemployment benefits. Naming Rolling Dumpsters as her last employer, my sister claimed she was laid-off. The notice indicated some measure of financial responsibility was to be assigned to the business. If there was any disagreement with the findings, supposedly I was entitled to submit written declaration, which I promptly did. According to information provided by the EDD, a hearing would be held before a final determination was to be reached. In my response I explicitly detailed the facts of the matter: The employee stole the company truck, refused communication, and abandoned her position. Subsequently, no hearing took place, at least none that I had been informed of, and the EDD's decision was to grant her unemployment benefits. I can only speculate regarding what happened, but I suspect strings got pulled somewhere. I really do not begin to believe something simply got overlooked. Both the business and myself personally had already been ongoingly targeted for a number of years. Satan's fiery darts had been launched once again with a precalculated, focused objective to steal, kill, and destroy – a fitting narrative.

When the union concocted a way to kick me out in January of 2002, I produced documentation to sufficiently refute their invented reasoning. There is no doubt in my mind that if I pursued the matter, I would have ended up dead. Rolling Dumpsters was growing significantly and was certainly going to make me a wealthy man. Thinking the union boys got what they wanted, I figured if I left it at that they would leave me alone and I would live to fish again another day. I was wrong, very wrong. The harassment was incessant, coming at me from every direction possible. I was constantly getting blindsided by some nefarious act somewhere. It just wore on me to the point where I figured I was going to end up dead anyway. In 2005 I called the F.B.I., thinking the feds must be able to lend assistance in some way. I even reasoned that they had to be aware of what was going on, at least to some extent. They must be watching these guys and are about ready to make a bust, I thought. The F.B.I. told me they were unwilling to help. According to them, any recourse I had was through California's state government agencies such as the Department of Consumer Affairs, they said. To me that would be like telling the fox the henhouse is being raided while the fox is dining on chicken. The union guys told me several years prior, "We pretty much have California locked up. We're going to take over the country." In 2007 I decided to make an exit. My attempts to sell the business as a whole received some interest, but nothing developed. In the interest of survival, I hastily sold off the equipment and got away from the industry altogether. Again I thought they would leave me alone. Again

I was wrong.

The church in La Crescenta had a Tuesday night prayer group that had been meeting regularly for many years. One night in 2007 as we were sharing requests before entering into our time of prayer, someone presented a prayer request for Delbert's attorney, Tom. I was acquainted with the husband-and-wife lawyer team which had been close friends with Delbert for many years. The person bringing up the matter stated that Tom was in the I.C.U. at the local hospital undergoing dialysis to remove toxins from his system. Within a few days he passed away. His wife Eva remained busy running the law office until 2016 when she died too. I had just called her at the office for legal advice, then the next thing I knew I was reading her obituary in a small local newspaper. Tom and Eva were very active politically, often hosting republican events at their home in La Cañada. As legal representation for Delbert and possessing staunch conservative values, they were prime targets for wicked individuals who possessed nothing but disdain for people like them. Any secret settlement agreement Delbert entered into in all probability involved Tom and Eva. The circumstances surrounding their passing I consider something more than simply mysterious; there is an uncanny resemblance to the indoctrination narrative divulged to me many years prior. Although I cannot prove any foul play, I do not begin to believe their passing was an accident.

In 2008 I learned about Dr. James Privitera, a nutritional specialist in Covina California. He had a strong reputation for treating patients battling various ailments including toxin exposure. This guy was a real whiz. He wrote books, taught seminars, appeared on television, and traveled far and wide in the process of helping countless people. He developed a procedure analyzing live blood under dark field microscopy. Recognized as an expert on the subject, he described to me factors that cause life-threatening clotting in human blood, which just so happens to include toxins. He even authored a book, *Silent Clots: Life's Biggest Killers*. As he was to so many others, Dr. Privitera became an advocate and hero to me as well.

The first time in his office I had a hair analysis performed which revealed the presence of a significant amount of both uranium and cadmium. When I informed him of how these toxic elements got there, he gave me kind of a sideways, skeptical look. Performing a live blood analysis, he pointed out on the monitor how I was experiencing an excessive amount of platelet aggregation. According to Dr. Privitera, this abnormal increase in blood clotting can be attributed to a variety of factors, including exposure to toxic substances. I continued to see him for many years, scheduling a visit each time something happened that caused me to fall ill. The same procedures would be performed each time and sure enough, poisons were found. On one visit when I was feeling absolutely terrible, he took a droplet of my blood, placed it on a glass slide, and inserted it under the microscope. Right away he looked at me and asked if I was feeling okay. I responded with the honest truth, then he asked if I had eaten anything that day which I had not. He gave me two capsules of a high-quality fish oil, waited a little less than half an hour, then retested. The clotting had been greatly reduced. He explained how fish oil is not only a potent blood thinner, but also dissolves clots, unlike pharmaceutical blood thinning medications. That is precisely why I received from him a doctor's prescription for fish oil.

After seeing this brilliant doctor for a few years I considered him my primary care physician. Between his analytical procedures and the prescribed treatments, I hold the opinion that God used him to save my life. Over time, the chronic reappearance of toxins stirred his curiosity and he became increasingly inquisitive about my circumstances. Slowly but surely, he believed what I had been telling him about the union guys and my involvement with them. He eventually became fully convinced, even directly stating so to me. If the opportunity ever arose to testify on my behalf in a court of law, then he would be my man. He would be the one who would take the stand and provide expert testimony. He would be the one who would say, 'I know what I'm talking about. This man is being poisoned!' Although I did consider this made him a target, I figured he really was not on the radar of those evildoers. That was until 2013.

I had a friend who had been a member of Christian Life Church for many years. He and I became buddies right away when I started attending in 1986. A year younger than myself, he has faced a life-long challenge with a certain disability. After his parents passed away, in-home care became necessary to assist him with his daily needs. Vincent and one other guy were regulars among several people pro-vided by government agencies. In 2008 I was brought in as well to help look after my friend, working there into 2009. He had a say-so regarding the choice of paid care providers, responding jovially at the proposition of me becoming one of them. I am not a difficult person to get along with, but Vincent and I did not exactly see eye-to-eye. It became evident to me that the people harassing me got to him. Arriving at the front door of my friend's home just a few days after I began, I heard conversation going on inside and waited at the door-step listening to what was being said. Vincent was attempting to con-vince him I am some kind of bad guy who he should part ways with. "You don't want another Freddy," Vincent said, referring to a previous caregiver who had stolen from him and his family, "Do you?" Vincent continued. My buddy replied with a hesitant and drawn out, "Well, No." I heard my name repeated in more than simply condescend-ing conversation. "He's not good for you!" Vincent asserted. Oddball things increasingly occurred at that home around Vincent as time went on. I initially held my tongue for the sake of peace in the home, but the shenanigans continued and I eventually spoke up, question-ing Vincent on a number of things. For the most part he denied in-volvement. When he was unmistakably responsible for something, he attempted to justify his actions with some silly explanation. In regards to some things, he outright sought to displace the blame onto me. It was clear he was not acting alone; somebody got to him. I considered it a confirmation of my suspicions when the California Department of Social Services began sending me documents indicating I was receiv-ing more income from the job than I actually had been. Addressing the matter with them, they deflected responsibility to another agency who deflected it again themselves with the whole thing ending up at the original starting gate. The carousel charade proved to be an endless dizzying cycle with no antidote. After government agencies finally assigned responsibility to my friend's family, my employment was terminated without compensation for the discrepancy.

Before it was all over, a diligent effort was made to terminate me in a more comprehensive capacity. One evening, as it was the caregiver's job, Vincent prepared a meal of shrimp and vegetables in some kind of sauce. Setting aside a bowl for me, he was insistent that I eat it. The offering, however, was clearly out of context; we already had issues between us and I did not trust him in the least. The bowl of food was subsequently placed in the refrigerator, supposedly there for me when I was ready for it, but there was absolutely no way I was ever going to eat it. The next day my friend wanted it, but Vincent exclaimed, "No, that's Mark's!" which aroused my suspicions all the more. The day after that a different caregiver came in. Complying with my buddy's requests, that man innocently heated up and served him that bowl of shrimp, vegetables, and sauce. When Vincent came in later that day and learned what happened, he was incensed. My friend went to bed that evening saying he was not feeling well. The following day he was admitted to the hospital. Staying there several days, he complained of some of the exact same symptoms I have experienced when I was poisoned. In exacting detail, he pointed to the center of his abdomen saying, "It's vibrating right here." As peculiar as that sounds, I have experienced precisely the same thing. Although certain conditions were identified, no specific cause was established for his condition. In consideration of these events, your perspective may be different than mine. I am thoroughly convinced about what happened; it all just fits the narrative.

When I again fell victim to poisoning in 2009, I found myself reluctant to return to the same emergency room where I had been before. Thinking I could avoid the ridicule I had previously been subjected to, I went to a different hospital where maybe they would at least lend some measure of credence to my explanation. Providing no diagnosis, they too were unable to identify any cause for my ailment. I fully expected the staff would be skeptical, that was a given, but I felt mocked once again when the emergency room physician told me, "I don't have a Geiger Counter!" Following up with Dr. Privitera, laboratory analysis revealed yet again a high level of uranium was present. This time I also tested exceptionally high for lead while cadmium was nearly off the chart. The results indicated a total toxic representation score of one hundred percent.

Throughout 2010 I lived in the parsonage on the property at the church in La Crescenta. If one thinks residing on holy ground affords full protection from evil, you had better think again. The harassment that had been assailing me for so many years followed me there too. One day while I was viewing sporting events on the computer, pornographic images appeared on the screen. I immediately got off that computer and notified Pastor Tim of what happened. It did not end there, though. Tools I had in the storage sheds were vandalized costing me at least a couple thousand dollars. Large groups of kids from the nearby high school began to congregate using our church property as a hangout. Evidence of drug use was left behind in their wake. One day after school, a large number of them gathered at the church to watch a fight between two boys which never materialized. From that point on the young people became prohibited from loitering on the property.

Then one night during May of that year, I was poisoned while sleeping in that parsonage. Each night I leaned a metal folding chair against the backdoor. Even though it was locked, if anyone somehow opened the door it would send the chair crashing down on the tile floor awakening me. The makeshift alarm served its purpose one night as I was awakened by the loud crash. I laid there as still as I could while waiting for an intruder to enter. Not making a sound, I laid awake for at least a half hour, ready to leap up and confront the person. Stupid me, I fell back asleep. I was later awakened by a liquid dropping onto my face and mouth. Bolting upright, I saw somebody flee out that backdoor. There was no way I could get up in pursuit quickly enough to catch the person. I had a terrible metallic taste in my mouth, so I washed it out along with my face as thoroughly as I could. Within in a few hours I began to feel ill. Before the day was over, I became very sick. My keys had been laying on the table beside where I was sleeping. The master key fitting many of the church locks was bent in a u-shape. Pastor Tim and I discovered several of the locks on the property had been damaged. That incident had me sick in bed for about three weeks. As a consequence, I got into the habit of placing my hand over my mouth when sleeping, something I subconsciously continue to do to this day. Sometimes I end up with a sore jaw the next day because of it.

Still reeling from the effects in October of that year, I paid a visit to Dr. Privitera. A toxicological lab test was performed once again revealing high levels of cadmium, lead, and uranium and a live blood analysis also showed excessive clotting. By now Dr. Privitera had become an impassioned advocate, coming to the realization there was actually truth to my preposterous claims of being poisoned.

Within a matter of weeks following that break-in, Pastor Tim submitted his notice of resignation. The reason cited was to give way to a pastor who he and the board felt could better lead the church through the rebuilding project. I suspected then and still do today that, although that may have been a reason, there was something more influencing his departure. Afterall, he and his wife had just purchased a home in the area. In our personal conversations, I informed Pastor Tim of the challenges I had been enduring for so long and about the workings of those union thugs. Much of what I told him he was beginning to witness for himself. He had been pastoring there at the time Delbert passed away, likely hearing a thing or two from him along the way. All this gave me reason to believe that Tim and his wife were simply getting the heck out of there for their own safety which makes perfect sense to me. He would not just state it outright though. Like Delbert, he held his tongue, furnishing me just one small glimpse beyond the façade saying, "I admire your ability to stand up to those guys." Not long after they left, I heard that she was battling blood clots. I had suspected perhaps they had fallen mysteriously ill themselves. Having a resource I only wish existed for me, Tim and Cheryl hightailed it out of California to a small town in Texas where a brother of his lives.

I formed lifelong friendships with several of the wonderful brethren at Christian Life Church. Among those were Cliff and Lou, a dear couple who were tremendous prayer warriors. Sometime around 2011, give or take a year, the three of us met with Cliff's cousin Roland. These lunch meetings became a regular thing and we all looked forward to them. On this particular occasion we met at Marie Callender's Restaurant in Pasadena. Rollie, as Cliff referred to him, had been a missionary in Israel and in the Philippines before retiring and he was quite a prayer warrior in his own right. Just like Cliff and Lou, he was an absolutely delightful person and I cherished every moment we spent together. The restaurant was completely empty that afternoon. As we entered, the hostess seated us to the left and we had the entire restaurant to ourselves. Soon after we arrived, what appeared to be a husband and wife couple came in. I watched as the hostess began to escort them the opposite direction, to the right. The man, looking over in our direction, pointed. The hostess then changed direction, walking over towards us. When they sat down just two tables away, the man was fiddling with what I thought was a still photo camera. He placed it on the table directly facing us, but it did not appear to me at the time he was taking pictures. Reflecting back upon it, I suspect that he was actually videotaping with that camera. A few minutes later a uniformed police officer stepped inside the front entrance. He looked around, spotted that couple, then walked over and sat with them. I was dumfounded as I immediately recognized that cop. I saw him at least twice before: once with the L.A. City councilman at the Mausoleum, then at the police station when I was reporting my stolen trailers. He was an L.A.P.D. officer in uniform, in Pasadena, and outside of his City of Los Angeles jurisdiction. Although I was concerned, to the best of my knowledge none of us fell ill from anything we consumed that day.

After we finished our meal inside, we moved our meeting to a patio area just outside the front door where the four of us engaged in an extended time of prayer. About half an hour later the three other lone patrons exited. Walking past us, the guy with the cameras directed a snide remark, "It's contagious!" It was unmistakably obvious he was unapproving of us four Christians exercising our sincerely held spiritual beliefs. Fortunately, they continued on their way while we continued in fellowship and prayer for at least another couple of hours. At one point I sat down surrounded by the three of them laying hands on me in prayer. During that time Rollie received a vision of me preaching to crowds, even in large stadiums filled with people. I have had similar spiritual visions myself. Perhaps that prophecy has already been fulfilled in ways that I do not see or maybe it is yet to come, I do not know. What I do know, however, is my heart became very heavy when not long after our meeting that day I was informed of Rollie's passing. That was the last time I saw him. He died suddenly and unexpectedly from a stroke.

During a portion of 2012 I was the maintenance man for an eighty-unit condominium complex in the San Fernando Valley. I later learned the lady who hired me worked on election campaigns for L.A. City councilmen and California state politicians, all democrats endorsed by union officials. Had I been afforded that knowledge beforehand, then I likely would have declined to work there. As it was, when arriving to work I placed my lunch and beverages in the refrigerator located in the kitchen of the recreation room. The room was always kept locked and I felt confident at the time in the safety of the items I was putting in there each workday. When I became ill that December, I identified that to be the most likely place where they got me.

It was Christmas Eve and my dad had been expecting me at his house. I was not only too sick to attend, but made yet another trip to the emergency room instead. Although my condition was quite severe, I was able to drive myself to the nearest hospital, one I had never been to before. It was notably crowded, but I was seen without waiting long. I was dressed in just the hospital gown and my underwear waiting in the examination room to be seen by the attending physician. It struck me as very out of the ordinary when he came in, rolled up to me in the short, wheeled swivel stool, and promptly pulled down my underwear. Dismissing the notion that he may have been gay, I thought maybe his actions had something to do with photographs that appeared in my grandparent's unoccupied mobile home in Porterville a few months prior.

Grandma and grandpa passed away six months apart in 2009, but Dad kept their home and he and I would often retreat there. On one particular visit I arrived to find a deep indentation in the kitchen floor that had not been there before. I also discovered Polaroid instant photos laying around inside that were taken of some man cutting off his penis with a long kitchen knife. Several photos taken in various stages were scattered all around, the final act depicting the severed object laying in a stainless-steel mixing bowl. There were several photos, but none showed his face. Where they came from or who put them there, I do not know, but somebody had been in the home. Whether or not the sickening event really occurred, I do not know either. I did tell a couple of people about the discovery and later burned all the photographs in a firepit.

Back in the E.R. I thought, 'Could this doctor somehow possess knowledge of those photos and assumed they were taken of me? Did he abruptly drop my underwear to confirm or rule out any suspicions? Why else would he be doing that? Inspecting my genitals had absolutely nothing to do with the symptoms I complained of. Whatever his reasoning, his physical exam ascertained that I do in fact have a penis, the very one God created me with.

Several tests were performed on me during that E.R. visit, but no causative factor was conclusively identified. I waited as laboratory blood test results were pending. "Your liver is angry," was their final determination. It felt like to me I had been ridiculed once again. I left there with my internal physiological processing plant angry, the remainder of me disgruntled, and a prescription for three or four medications. After paying for parking, I made my way up to Porterville where I would attempt to recover.

Over the next few days my condition worsened. Wrapping myself in a blanket and laying directly on top of the heater vent, I just could not get warm. Tylenol failed to bring my fever under control. My brain was not functioning well at all and I began to experience what I can only describe as strange shivering fits. The nearest person I knew, Uncle Weldon, was 40 miles away. For three days I asked him to come over and take me to the hospital. He said if I was that bad, then I should call an ambulance. The reality is that I was that bad and should have called 911, but I was not in my right mind. He finally did come and we made the jaunt over to the local hospital in Porterville. Just like the other one a week or so prior, the E.R. waiting room was crowded. After being triaged I was promptly whisked into an examination room where a barrage of tests and questions were hurled at me. They were puzzled by my description of the shivering fits, but their puzzlement did not last long because I began to go into another one right there and they got to see it for themselves. Weldon backed away as staff and equipment moved rapidly all around me. A medication was injected into my I.V. access as I was circling the drain. I do not know how long it lasted, but when I came to, a male nurse standing beside my bed said, "That was weird!" I thought so too and had been struggling to communicate that to them. The turbulence appeared to be over as I felt like I was in smoother flight. Weldon, standing bedside, expressed remorse for not taking me in sooner. "They're going to admit you," he said. There were no available beds, but I was in bad enough condition that they were going to make room for me somewhere. It turned out that I was even worse off than any of us thought. The laboratory results revealed, "You are in hepatic and renal failure," I was informed. When I said that I was circling the drain, I was not kidding; I nearly lost my life this time around. My liver and kidneys were shutting down. As far as I am concerned that is a stark contrast to, "Your liver is angry," the diagnosis I received from the other E.R. just days prior.

A variety of tests were performed during my two-week stay in the telemetry unit. In that hospital I felt like I was finally being listened to and cared about, all except for one specialist. He was rather insistent that I confess to being an I.V. drug user. The deep vein thrombosis in my liver's portal vein, according to him, could only be attributed such a cause. Numerous diagnostic imaging procedures ultimately produced this finding located in the main blood vessel draining my liver. At that time, the extent of my drug use entailed a cup or two of coffee each morning, occasional iced tea, and something for pain only as needed. Illegal drug use was in no way part of my repertoire and I have always possessed an aversion to needles. Never in my life have I ever injected anything into my veins nor allowed another to do so outside of the medical profession. If I attempted to, then I would undoubtedly experience the same vasovagal effect I have experienced on numerous occasions when donating blood. I am not certain if that one doctor ever believed me or not and I really do not care either way. What I am certain of is, I had a toxin-induced blood clot that could have taken my life at any moment and nearly did.

Since I was nearly two hundred miles away from home during that hospital stay in Porterville, Weldon was the only family or friend who came to visit me that whole time. A pastor from a church I visited nearby came to see me two or three times and I very much appreciated our time of prayer together. Before exiting the room following our last visit, Pastor Peter said, "I love you." I do not know the man, but he was sincere in saying that. Fighting for my life all alone in a hospital far from home, it meant a lot for me to hear those words.

The staff at Sierra View Medical Center exhibited hearts of compassion towards their patients leaving a positive imprint on me regarding the quality of care I received at that facility. One nurse advised me to keep activated charcoal on hand to have readily available in the event of a recurrence. He further explained how he watched the telemetry monitors at the nurse's station during the night shifts and observed my pulse rate drop exceedingly low while I was sleeping. "I wondered if you were going to make it," he said. One may say that

I did make it, but as I have learned the hard way, my life is in God's hands. It is not a matter if I make it, rather it is for God to determine when I go Home. He has numbered my days. As children of God we are assured that all the days ordained for us were written in His book before even one of them came to be (Psalm 139:16b). The words of the Apostle Paul find fertile ground in the soil of my heart: "For to me, to live is Christ and to die is gain" (Philippians 1:21). I have come to know with all certainty, the worse thing they can do to me is the best thing that can happen to me. Through it all, God has made it distinctly clear that He has work for me to do; I am not going home yet.

Back at grandparent's mobile home, I eventually recovered enough to make the drive back to Los Angeles. I then plotted a direct course to Dr. Privitera's office. Even though I would rather it be under different circumstances, I enjoyed seeing this man who became my friend. He was hero to many and that, for good reason. This time the results exposed the highest level of uranium I had ever exhibited on a toxin panel. It was his stated opinion that the supplements he had me taking, including the turmeric I added on my own, saved my life. According to what he told me, had I not been taking these things, the poisons would have proved fatal this time around. I cannot begin to disagree knowing exactly what I felt in my own body.

I had nearly been eradicated from the face of the earth and it took quite some time to recover. Besides seeing Dr. Privitera after this attempt on my life, I also paid a few visits to L.A. County medical facilities. That began with a seeing a primary care doctor who conducted some tests. Prothrombin time and protein C factors did not indicate blood coagulation abnormalities. Rejecting my explanation, they appeared bent on a search for somewhere else to assign blame. Laboratory tests failed to support their quest and I was referred to the county hospital for further evaluation. I watched as a lady there was handed my chart. Identifying herself as a student physician in residency, she took a hasty glance at the first two pages of my documents. Without bothering to carefully look over my chart or examine laboratory results she said, "This has to be Valley Fever. Have you been to the Central Valley?" That was the moment I became suspicious. Porterville is in California's Central Valley, but she had no way of knowing I had been up there. Besides, Sierra View Medical Center would most certainly have discovered any microbial infection including Valley Fever. My gentle answers were in no way reciprocated in like manner. "This has to be fatty liver then," was her next conclusion. My conclusion, however, was to terminate my status as a patient with their health care system. Not only was I repeatedly spoken to condescendingly, but they acted as if I was blaming them for the murder attempt. They were not defendants; we were not in a court of law. Why did they act this way? Considering what I experienced with their L.A. County healthcare system, I figured they were just going to conclude whatever could be pulled out of their hats. In that defensive approach, they could simply write whatever they wanted to in my medical charts. If they wanted it to be fatty liver, then my assigned diagnosis would reflect that. The truth be told, any hepatic dysfunction may by all means be a consequence of a liver damaged via ingested toxins. Resulting impacts may include the liver's ability to metabolize fats, carbohydrates, and proteins. The liver is the processing plant of the human body; everything circulating in our bloodstream must go through it including any poisons present. Such things inflict significant harm on the liver. A drunk person is an intoxicated person – a person with a substance, though intentionally consumed, that is toxic to the liver. Alcoholics may die as a result of liver damage; cirrhosis of the liver for instance.

Dr. Privitera appeared healthy and energetic as usual when I visited him following my near-death experience. He exercised regularly, playing tennis in addition to other activities. I dropped in his usually bustling office a few weeks later to pick up a few supplements, but there was an unsettling silence about the place. "He died!" one of the nurses told me with an unnerving tone. I was absolutely shocked. My jaw dropped, but nothing came out of my mouth as I just stared at her and she at me. Clearly Dr. Privitera's entire staff held those identical sentiments. At the time of this writing, it has been almost nine years since that highly esteemed medical doctor departed from among us. One can still read opinions posted on the internet from people who believe Dr. Privitera's death was not an accident. Several years prior I realized he was a potential target. None of those people posting on-line, however, have any knowledge of who I am let alone the circumstances I have faced. I share the same opinion with them, but how could I ever begin to prove anything. The events, the timing, and the fact that he would be my most credible witness all combine to point to a logical conclusion: He was knocked off. I am not the only one who thinks so. I believe it is much more than simply circumstantial conjecture – it just fits the narrative.

In September of 2013 I rented a home in La Crescenta and knew it would be just a matter of time before they would come after me there too. Finding most of the neighbors to be friendly, I befriended a few even doing handyman work at some of their homes. It did not take long for one particular neighbor to become compromised though, as things became clear the man living immediately adjacent on one side became radicalized in the efforts to destroy me. It was obvious they had gotten to him as he began doing things attempting to provoke me. There was a demonic component to it as well, evidenced by a terribly atrocious odor – the stench of decaying flesh filling the air. Confronted by it one day when walking outside, I vocally asserted authority over every devil, demon, and evil spirit, commanding them to flee. The disgusting odiferous presence instantly disappeared, but re-manifested itself a few days later. I was not the only one to notice it either. My landlord resided in the front house and was hosting a birthday celebration one day. I watched as one of her visitors detected a foul stench. "That's a corpse!" he exclaimed as he began searching all around the vicinity. Thinking he would locate a dead animal, he discovered nothing. I knew right away what was going on and I never said a word about it to him. Nobody else could smell it at all, but he was overcome by it and was perplexed by his failure to locate the source.

Living in that little back house for six years, a number of adverse experiences occurred. Twice on that little side street while coming home, a small white car traveling the opposite direction suddenly accelerated and veered directly towards me, much like the great mirror capers from a few years prior. This time, I believe the objective was to cause me to collide with parked vehicles while swerving to avoid an accident. The second time it happened I actually did swipe against a parked car and had to file a claim with my insurance company. I suspect it was the same person in the same white car each time and on both occasions it was clearly deliberate. There was no way I was going to be able to reverse course to commence pursuit quickly enough in my older automobile. I could only watch in my mirror as they sped away.

While I was living at that residence, several electronic devices I owned in addition to every single appliance inside got fried. Most of the items were plugged into surge protectors and the appliances were running off of G.F.I. protected electrical outlets. If it all happened at once, then a plausible explanation might be presented. The incidents occurred, however, over a several year span, wiping out one item at a time. One night I was awakened from my sleep by a buzzing electrical feeling on my leg which was touching the wall. I moved my leg only to have the sensation follow. I moved my leg all around, then placed my hands on the wall and whatever it was continued. There was not a window in that area where I could look outside and to access the exterior would involve scaling two fences. If I did, then I would end up in the backyard of that one particular neighbor they got to. I could never get around there in time to catch anybody in the act of doing something. I made my way out there anyway, but found nothing. The following day I was appallingly goofy in the head, much like from toxin exposure. The symptoms persisted for a few weeks before gradually tapering off. From that day on, my bed was as far away from any wall in that home as I could get it. One might begin to suggest certain electrical problems existed in that structure. If the fried electrical items were limited to within that dwelling, then I might begin to believe that may have been the case.

After the first incident with that little white car on my street I purchased a dash cam. I familiarized myself with it and figured I found a way to adequately afford myself some protection. That did not last long though. One day I went out to my vehicle parked on the street in front of the house and discovered several electrical problems which were not there when I drove it just the day before. The cruise control was fried and several lights no longer functioned. I checked and replaced several bulbs and fuses, but not everything worked again. A motive certainly existed for somebody to cause the damage: the new dash cam was completely fried as well. About a year and a half before I moved out of that home, I parted ways with that automobile and acquired a used minivan to replace it. All electrical controls functioned flawlessly in that van, but that changed within a short time as the exact same thing happened to it too.

The six years I rented that little back house saw a fair share of challenges. There were a couple of neighbors who were watchful and that likely kept things from being worse than they were. One neighbor who lived there a long time suggested that I should be careful about trusting in my landlord. I had already begun to suspect some of the weird things happening were intentional and she was receiving some kind of compensation in the process. Several years before I ever lived there, another man spoke negatively about the lady, but I really did not believe him at the time. Once that neighbor spoke up though, I realized it was time for me to hightail it out of there. Pieces of a puzzle fell together illustrating a picture: She had pleaded with me to rent the place from her. Although I was adamantly resistant, that did not dissuade her insistence that she would not rent the place to anybody other than me. That process continued for about three months before she finally offered a deal that was too good to pass up. Along the way, I learned she had a family member who was employed as a police officer – the same man who smelled the stench at the party. In retrospect, it seems my landlord stood to profit from my presence. I think she knew all along what was going on and saw an opportunity to profit by renting the place to me. I had known this woman many years and held her in some measure of esteem, but left there seriously recalculating my perspective. I parted ways more amicably than I would expect to see from someone else in my position. When I moved out, she owed me money, but never paid it. I left the home in immaculate condition, completely ready for another tenant to move in. Input from additional people after I moved out solidified my conclusions. Two people who attended the same church as her for several years informed me of certain values she holds which are things I find troubling. Then a former pastor said some things that did not exactly reflect well upon my former landlord. The words of those union boys from several years prior have come back to haunt me over and over again: "Everyone has their price. Some just cost more than others. We divide people. We cut them off from everyone and they end up all alone." Offered enough money, it is astounding to me how many people will throw you under the bus. Many have sought to profit even if meant stepping over my dead body to grab that fistful of dollars and it has been going on for a long time – I am counting in the decades now. Friendships are willingly discarded in bowing down to the almighty dollar.

God blessed me beyond measure by giving me the best man I have ever known as my own father. He was genuinely kind and unreasonably forgiving. I could not have asked for a better dad. He was always the one person I could turn to, especially during the challenging times I have faced in life. After an honorable discharge from the U.S. Army in the early 1960s, Dad went to work for the telephone company, devoting nearly half a century of his life to that job. I kept Dad well apprised of my difficulties, informing him of virtually every minute detail. A few years before passing away in 2015, he began to experience some of the exact same symptoms I have endured. I repeatedly suggested he get tested, but Dad really did not like seeing doctors for any reason. He kept his suffering to himself for the most part, but I was able to squeeze a little out of him here and there. It was evident to me they got to him; I became thoroughly convinced of it. Although he reluctantly made a few visits to some doctors, the subject of being poisoned was never addressed. I tried to get him to see

Dr. Privitera, but he never did go. He was undoubtedly fearful of being judged a fool if he suggested he was being poisoned. That was the same initial concern I had; it was a fear I had to overcome. Dad said he wanted to keep working a few more years, but lethargy just took everything out of him, so he retired a little early. I watched as my own dad was being victimized and it did not appear there was anything I could do about it. One day out of nowhere in October of 2015, Dad suddenly turned orange. His brain was terribly squirrely and he was not himself. My jaundiced dad, experiencing liver failure, was taken to the emergency room. When I walked in, the doctor asked dad, "Do you know who that is?" "That's my son," came Dad's reply as looked up at me with pinpoint pupils. That E.R. doctor then proceeded to examine him, palpating his lower abdomen. She looked up at me and out of her mouth came the last words I ever wanted to hear, "I'm sorry." An injection was given to help his kidneys process and eliminate toxins, but it only caused him to fade out of consciousness for the final time. Dad was admitted, then moved to a hospice unit within the same hospital the following day. Two days later I stood by his side and watched as he took his very last breath in this world. No autopsy was performed, but nevertheless the cause of death was listed as cancer. They thought it was a fast-acting aggressive form and questioned why he did not feel anything or complain. Nobody knew, including Dad himself. Next to Jesus Christ, my dad was my number one hero in all of life. Now he was gone. I had my suspicions for several years leading up his departure. Afterall, it just fit the narrative.

My dad was just one of three people I lost in 2015, those three being the closest to me at the time. I lived with my friend Veatus throughout most of 2009. Albeit she was in her eighties, I remain unconvinced her rapid cognitive decline occurred in the natural order of things. Twice I arrived at her home to find somebody inside sitting on her couch talking with her who she did not even know. On both occasions, the person made a quick departure following my appearance while avoiding my questions in the process. In the bedroom where I had been sleeping, I found an empty capsule on the carpet under the dresser where I kept nutritional supplements. It was an exact match with one of those supplements, so I threw away everything I had that could have been adulterated. Veatus was 93 when her time came, but I have never been confident that time came unhastened.

Cliff left us in December of 2015, a year or so after his wife Lou passed. I stayed with them part-time for about three years beginning in 2011. A ridiculous number of goofy things happened at their home as well, which just seemed like par for the course. Lou also underwent rapid cognitive decline. Although at the time I considered it natural progression, in retrospect I have realized it fits the narrative.

Veatus, Cliff, and Lou were all up there in years. If it were not for all the other things that happened around us, then I would be less suspicious. When we live into our eighties or nineties the inevitable looms nigh. Just like my dear friend Delbert who knew he was being poisoned, their ages made them an easy target. The passing of Veatus, Cliff, and Lou may be more readily dismissed compared to some of the others. A person may suggest it occurred in the natural course of events, but I am not convinced. Their stories fit like puzzle pieces into the bigger picture; it just fits the narrative.

Uncle Weldon was my mom's younger brother. He was 11 years older than me and was much like a brother in many ways. After I first fell ill in 2004 and 2005, Weldon came to live with me and helped run the business. Although I made him acutely aware that he was now a target, Weldon figured he could sufficiently avoid anything they could attempt to throw at him. From that point we committed more time to our relationship, even more so after I walked away from the motion picture industry altogether at the end of 2007. Then came the call in May of 2017. Weldon was diagnosed with advanced stage esophageal cancer. I dropped everything and drove up to Central California to be with him. Radiation and chemotherapy treatments had already begun in the battle against what doctors described as an aggressive form of cancer. Before long, oncologists identified malignancies. It was subsequently arranged for Weldon to receive in-home hospice care. I was with him to the end, utilizing my experience in healthcare to provide for the needs of a loved one. Another painful loss, Uncle Weldon left us in June 2017 at the age of 61. Did he contract cancer apart from any criminal activity introducing a causative agent? Those union guys spoke of their targets suddenly falling victim to aggressive forms of cancer. I cannot definitively answer the unresolved questions, but I can say that it just seems to fit the narrative.

Dr. Jerry Jones was my mentor and close friend for many years. Holding two ministerial doctorates, the man served the Lord nearly 70 years, from age sixteen to his homegoing at 86. His father was also a minister, building and pastoring churches before moving on and repeating the process. It is difficult to get close to a man like him. They are usually so preoccupied that there is no opportunity for one-on-one engagement with common parishioners. That was not the case between Pastor Jerry, PJ, and I. Besides sitting under his teaching steadily for nearly a decade and a half, I did a lot of work at his house. We drove to Mississippi together for a Thanksgiving getaway at his brother's where we got to fish for three days straight. Whenever he had a speaking engagement or filled in for another pastor, I would often be there at his side. PJ considered me much like a son, expressing concern to others in the infrequent event of my absence from our weekly Bible study.

The challenges I have endured for so long is something PJ was well aware of. Like others, he was at skeptical at first, but eventually witnessed enough himself to become convinced. My hospitalization in January of 2013 had a strong impact on him. All along the way PJ could see our Gracious Father's hand was upon me, observing evidence of His calling. If ever I was in a courtroom and needed the testimony of somebody who could ascertain this truth, then he was my man. That made him a target. Out of concern for my close friend, I informed him so a number of times. PJ's reaction was always to slough it off, saying he considered himself somewhat impervious to evil. Awarded a key to the City of Burbank, he viewed himself as being on good graces with all people regardless of political affiliation. In the work of ministry, Dr. Jones was always quick to deflect discussion away from political party interests, instead shifting the focus to God's Kingdom. One year I attended the City of Burbank's annual mayor's prayer breakfast with him where he was a regular attendee. When ceremonies were conducted in observation of various holidays, the City of Burbank called upon his services. Pastor Jerry told me he attended a breakfast meeting with the local congressional representative, Adam Schiff. PJ was a prominent figure, known by many and like by most. I think he not only underestimated our ancient foe, however, but both of us miscalculated the abundance of God's provision for him as well. Scripture tells us it is a privilege to suffer for Christ's sake. I think that is precisely what God had in mind when Pastor Jerry received a martyr's reward in Heaven. After devoting his entire life to ministering the Gospel of Jesus Christ, the circumstances that led to his departure endowed my dear friend with an increase in the compensatory package he received after crossing over Jordan into the Promised Land. A robe, a crown, and a bountiful reward awaited my dear friend.

On Sundays after church, PJ regularly made a forty-five-mile drive to be with his lady friend, Doris. That Sunday in early January of 2018 would be no different, but it would be his last. Somewhere around midway he stopped for fuel and began to experience the effects from blood clotting. He was able to make it the remainder of the way out to Doris's. From there he was taken to the hospital where he experienced further clotting. Two or three days later, after his adult children came in from all over the United States, the decision was made to pull the plug on life support systems. My pastor and dear friend was gone, suddenly and unexpectedly. In the normal course of life these things do happen. Considering the entirety of the situation, however, I am a little bit more than simply suspicious. These circumstances coupled with a special gift from God to PJ at the conclusion of his lifetime of faithful service provide all the convincing proof I need to say that it just fits the narrative.

Later that same year I traveled to the Philippines in connection with a ministry we supported through Dr. Jones. Our group wanted to continue that support, so I was to be our new representative, picking up where PJ left off. I had felt a tug in that direction for quite some time, pondering the possibility of making the trip well before PJ left us. Once I was down there, unexpected doors of ministry flew open before me. I had no way of seeing it coming: Newfound opportunities took hold of me as I realized a calling from God in that gloriously beautiful archipelago over 7,000 miles away. Dr. Jones visited a there few times himself making his first trip in the mid-1990s. Besides our Friday night Bible study group, people all over the United States and even into Canada supported PJ's ministry. At the time of his departure, a portion of that money was being allocated towards the construction of a church building in a Philippine province 160 miles north of Manila. Our combined monthly funding was consistently sent with the goal of gradually seeing the project come to complete fruition.

When I returned from that trip, plans were in the making for an extended return. A long-delayed foot surgery was finally scheduled, temporarily interrupting those plans. Then the COVID-19 pandemic came upon us further postponing my missionary campaign. At first, we continued to send a monthly contribution, but after a few short months a strange communication breakdown occurred. I became uncertain the money we were sending was actually making it to the intended recipient, Pastor Oscar. When his wife initiated contact via an online texting app, not only was I uncomfortable with that, but it seemed really out of place. Whether it was actually her or somebody filching her identity, incoming text messages claimed Oscar was no longer using email. I emphasized the importance of communication taking place directly between he and I, but to no avail. At about the time contact was severed they had suddenly procured resources from some other source sufficient to complete the entire building project all at once. Oscar's bother-in-law, Christopher, was a tremendous help to me during my visit. He was helping me plan some of the details of my return, then suddenly poof! Our communication was severed. One of the very last communications I received indicated other plans were being made: plans for Christopher's memorial service and burial. I do not think he even reached 30 years of age. The highest cost of living is dying, that is one everybody pays. The bill just arrives sooner for some than it does others. Answers have proven elusive regarding exactly what happened in any of this mess. Perhaps your guess is as good as mine. What I can tell you with all certainty, however, is that it just fits the narrative.

The foot surgery had been delayed time after time. I needed it for several years just as Dr. Rupp said I would more than 20 years prior when he performed the same procedure on my other foot. This time around my healthcare coverage was acquired through the State of California's exchange which was set up in conjunction with Obamacare. Much to my dismay, their plan would not permit me to see Dr. Rupp and I was assigned to another podiatrist, Allen Massihi. At nearly the last minute, Massihi rescheduled the procedure, postponing it a few days. After the surgery was performed, I had a couple of post-operative office visits with him. Massihi was insistent I was not to remove the dressing myself. When he redressed it in his office, I could see my large toe was completely out of place. I was instructed to return to his office a few months later, but that was simply not acceptable to me. I phoned in, made an appointment, and appeared in his office a few days following the last visit we had. In my conversation with his staff I had told them he needed to take a better look. My foot was completely bare when he entered the examination room. Massihi sat on the rolling stool and wheeled up to me. "What do you want me to see?" he inquired. Directing his attention to my foot, "My toe is rotated and moved over to the side," came my seemingly unnecessary response. The deformation resulting from the operation he performed was something nobody could miss. "There's nothing in the procedure that would cause the toe to rotate," Massihi responded as he stood, turned, and walked to the door. The man looked back one last time and asked, "Do you need any more anti-inflammatories?" "No," I replied, then he disappeared.

When I contacted my insurance company again, they would still not allow me to see Dr. Rupp. They informed me I was entitled to one second opinion under their coverage and that being from their list of approved providers. When I visited the second podiatrist they arranged for me to see, his nurse conducted an initial examination and was appalled at my explanation. "This should not have happened," she said. As she explained to me, her prior experience as supervisor of a surgical clinic equipped her with enough understanding to know better. The opinion of the nurse in that podiatrist's office did not corroborate with what I was told afterwards. That doctor proceeded to tell me he was personal friends with Massihi and that I should go back and allow him to continue caring for me. According to him, a bone fusion would be required to remedy the issue with my foot. After hearing what he had to say, I did not return to him either.

The negligence exhibited by the insurance company and both podiatrists was atrocious. To me it seemed a clear-cut case of medical malpractice. I did not view the matter as an opportunity to profit; I just wanted my foot fixed properly. Although I would be hard pressed to ever prove it, I honestly suspect the botched job was no accident. I consulted with lawyer after lawyer only be to told the same thing each time. The governor and state law makers in California had recently made changes to medical malpractice laws, leaving me little to no recourse. Another coincidence? I somehow find myself doubtful and am once again left with unanswered questions.

Coming to the end of my rope, I finally paid out of my own pocket for an office visit with Dr. Rupp. He was amazed at my dilemma, pointing out that Massihi not only screwed up the large toe on my right foot, but also the second toe on the other. The procedures were done at the same time and should have been routine, but evidently that was not the case for Massihi. Demand for compensation letters I sent to his office went unanswered. Dr. Rupp performed successful remedial surgery on both toes about a year after Massihi's butcher job. I personally assumed the cost which was several thousand dollars. The alternative was to live out the remainder of my life in this world maimed by Allen Massihi assisted by Obamacare and Covered California. Or was it the other way around? Either way, it fits the narrative.

The Obamacare insurance I obtained through the State of California proved deficient in even more ways. A flood of billing statements began pouring in after the surgery, the majority of them for services I did not receive. A wide variety of office visits and treatments were indicated on the medical invoices. There was even one for endocrinology, demonstrating remarkable creativity in the invented ploy. I have never seen an endocrinologist in my entire life. The insurance company either rejected payment or failed to pay and I was being held responsible. Between the hospital, their doctors, and the insurance company, I was on the phone constantly attempting to rectify the fabricated dilemma. One party displaced blame onto another who then deflected it yet again. I have no doubt it was a concocted scheme intentionally designed to provoke me. A billing company eventually admitted to committing several errors, but provided no further explanation. That also did not stop the additional bills from service providers which continued to arrive in my mailbox. Before they were finished, the circus act required countless hours of my time not to mention the aggravation involved in disputing the claims and that was not even the grand finale performed by those big top circus clowns. One more high wire deed was still hiding up their sleeves as evidenced by a manufactured malady with the pharmacy. When one of my prescriptions was initially filled, I received the correct medication as was the case with the first one or two refills. Afterwards, they tried giving me the wrong medication not just once, but several times over. After several failed attempts they claimed they were unable to provide the item as prescribed, but had no problem doing so before. Then on several successive visits they claimed my insurance had been canceled. About half a dozen times they had me waiting in the drug store while supposedly ironing out the problem by telephone. After two or three of these encounters, they began to place the blame on their computer system. When they could not do that any longer it became the insurance company's fault. According to the insurance company the issue was with the pharmacy. It seems I have read this script before: Round and round we go, where it stops nobody knows.

The script appears to fit right into the narrative.

When those operating motor vehicles around us do unwise things, with all reasonability it can be considered status quo. These things are something many of us have just come to expect. For the most part, I dismiss them as simply part of the mundane experience of driving in Southern California; these things just happen. With time and experience, I have become adept at foreseeing and avoiding many of the mistakes I see other drivers make. In the past few years, incidents involving other motorists often came at me in waves. At times I found myself inundated, like at that 118 Freeway to Interstate 5 connector. There were the occasions when it was easy to see certain things were intentional. Still, I pretty much just hang back and give a wide berth for things to happen, intentional or not. Such was the case in August of 2020 when I drove into the parking lot of a supermarket near my home. A young man came barreling down an alley straight at me and I immediately took notice, considering the possibility I was his predetermined target. I made an abrupt turn and headed to the opposite end of the parking lot. I had a notion he was targeting me and I intended to keep as far away as I could. In the back corner of the lot I stopped as a car was backing out of a parking spot. That fellow drove all the way around and came up behind me and began laying on the horn while wildly flailing his arms around. I decided I was just going to exit and get out of there as quickly as I could, but was stuck waiting for my chance. Before I could make the move, he exited his vehicle, came up to my window shouting obscenities, then spit in my face. Not many years prior that would have been a very ugly scene, but I managed to retain complete composure which only enraged him all the more. Muttering in prayer, I actually smiled at him. Racial slurs furiously flew from his mouth and I could sense a demonic presence. I thought to myself, I am a minister, I cannot react as the flesh dictates. I felt the Lord's calming presence settle down upon me accompanied by His impenetrable hedge of protection. The efforts of the man and his demons proved futile. When the opportunity presented itself, I departed. Not that I was happy about what happened, but I was proud of myself for not fighting evil with evil. To the best of my knowledge, I had never seen that man before and I have not seen him since.

The Tuesday evening prayer group at the church in La Crescenta had been well attended for many years, but eventually the numbers began to dwindle. My friend Barbara came to be the leader and at times it was only her and I meeting. She was a delightful lady who was quick to take your needs before the Lord in prayer. It was no different for me as she was well aware of my long-endured challenges. She prayed fiercely against the works of darkness relentlessly pestering me. During our prayer time she specifically prayed for recollection of adverse experiences to be erased from my memory. She had me curious about praying that way. I figure calling to mind things from the past equips us in such a way so as to avoid repeat occurrences. My questions to her regarding this were met with, "Just trust me." Barbara worked in a beauty shop and cut my hair for several years. Every single time I offered to pay her and every single time she refused. After I had been part of a different congregation for a few years, I paid a visit to the church in La Crescenta where I was informed of Barbara's recent passing. I was told it was a fast-acting aggressive form of kidney cancer which took her life a short time after diagnosis. I have lost a few loved ones along the way wherein the circumstances did not seem quite right. Then there were those times when I knew things were not right. Barbara was a dear friend, an advocate of my situation, and a devoted prayer partner. That was enough to make her a target. There will undoubtedly come a day when I will know for sure. Until then I am left to say, it just fits the narrative.

Pine Mountain Club is a small community in the mountains about 75 miles north of the San Fernando Valley. The clean air at that high elevation is a welcome retreat from the densely populated hustle and bustle of the urbanized areas in Los Angeles. I lived there part-time from October of 2019 to September of 2021. That beautiful place afforded me a measure of safety and solace from all the nasty things I have withstood, at least at the beginning. There were the expected things on the road you would encounter anywhere else and learn to tolerate, although way up there such occurrences were very few. Twice on the way up I found myself behind a vehicle being driven by someone who appeared impaired and both times I decided to just follow as they both arrived to their destinations without causing an accident. I found greater satisfaction in taking that approach rather than calling 911. If I did, who knows what may have happened (or not happened) to them or me.

Then something happened on the morning of April 30, 2021 that was unquestionably purposeful. Leaving early on that Friday morning, I was headed down to L.A. to meet with a friend. Approaching a stop sign on the steep residential street not far from the house, I noticed a man in the driveway of a corner house at that intersection. Standing there with the open car door, he looked directly at me as if he had been waiting just for me. As soon as he laid eyes upon me, he quickly jumped into that silver Chevy Volt and hastily backed out of the short driveway. I yielded a wide swath as I took all of the opposite lane in circumnavigating his belligerent maneuver. His strategy did not develop as planned and he proceeded towards the main highway taking a different route than me. Knowing I was on a slightly shorter route, I accelerated so I could get way ahead of him. Approximately four miles into the journey my get-away plan became hindered by a slower moving vehicle, but I figured I had put adequate distance behind me. A few minutes later the dude came flying up behind me as if he had another trick up his sleeve. He unexpectedly behaved himself as we drove three cars in a row for about 15 miles to Frazier Park where I activated my left turn indicator and proceeded to make a left turn where I was going to fuel my van. Without warning, that foolish man abruptly overtook me on the left side, driving across the solid double yellow line at the very moment I was conducting my turn, nearly causing a collision. I pulled into the fueling station on the other side of the pumps from him, exited my vehicle, then calmly and politely told him I did not appreciate him placing person and property in harm's way. "I was about to run out of gas," came his pugnacious reply. It was obvious he sought an escalation, but in no way was I about to play myself right into the hands of evil. "That was a foolish move," was my second and parting comment. Not satisfied with my refusal to argue, he was not done yet. "It would've been a lot worse if I would've run out of gas in the intersection," he claimed. I obtained three photographs of him and his vehicle as I disengaged the encounter without further ado.

When that guy left the gas station that morning, he turned right at the intersection, heading back the direction from where we came. As I replayed the events over and over in my mind, I knew I had crossed paths with him somewhere before, but could not recall when and where. The things he said could not be substantiated either because we passed two filling stations driving down the mountain that 15 miles. The first was right there in Pine Mountain Club about a mile downhill from the place where he first backed out on me. There was another about three miles before the one we pulled into. Besides all that, the car was a Chevy Volt which is a hybrid or electric vehicle. What he had to say about his malevolency ascertained the conduct was deliberate and premeditated. Meanwhile, I knew I had seen this guy somewhere before, but where?

Several months before that incident took place, there was a commotion up at the house in Pine Mountain Club. In what is a very quiet community, I heard a car peeling out in dirt and gravel and thought someone was having difficulty making it up a neighbor's steep driveway. About a minute later I heard the same sound again in a different driveway. From that window where I had been listening, I watched as a small silver car rounded the corner coming up our street, pulled into the next-door neighbor's driveway, and began to spin the tires throwing dirt and small rocks onto the roadway. I got a brief look at the driver and jotted down the license plates on a small note pad as he drove away. The guy came back and did the same thing again a couple of weeks later. There were also several occasions when I returned home to discover the exact same thing had occurred in our driveway. Looking around the area, I took notice that a few driveways had evidence somebody had done the same there as well. All of these places were in close proximity to the home where I was residing. After the run in with that fellow on the road, I searched for that 3-inch square piece of paper I had recorded the license plates on, but was unable to find it right away. It eventually turned up at a time I was not looking for it and guess what? The license plate was exactly the same as the one I photographed in the gas station that morning on April 30th, 2021. It just kind of fits the narrative, don't you think?

Throughout all my experiences I have found it too easy to become complacent and let my guard down. After months go by and nothing happens, my vigilant watchful eye begins to wane. You would think I would be more careful and not leave myself vulnerable, but I have done so too many times. Besides getting the right people into place, I believe that is one of the reasons the union guys said that it takes time to execute their schemes; they know their victims become less careful as time passes. Such was the circumstance when I returned to Los Angeles from Bowling Green Kentucky in September of 2021. For the first day, I thought I was just tired from the trip and was recovering. By the second or third day I knew I had been poisoned again. I became very ill, knowing I received a significantly large dose of whatever toxic cocktail was served up this time. Just like the other times, my symptoms were punctuated by an acute and severe squirrelly-in-the-head experience. Placing a large order for supplements that have been helpful to me in the past, I went after it as aggressively as I could. Based upon my symptoms, I believed uranium was the agent employed. When I tested about 30 days later, uranium and lead showed notably high, but cadmium was at an extraordinary level. This time I was traveling; I really should have been alert and cautious, but I let my guard down enough for them to get to me. Could it be that Barbara's prayer about erasing certain memories was affirmatively answered? Did I forget what the union boys said about nailing people when they travel just so that I would be nailed and they would be exposed? I know I was poisoned and it was the second that year. I also know it fits the narrative.

The things I have been through and continue to endure equates to nothing short of being beaten on a daily basis. It feels all the same if not worse. In fact, I would much rather be physically beaten every single day of my life than be subjected to this. One might expect government to protect someone in my shoes, but many among them are actually the facilitators of and participants in the wickedness. If I schemed and plotted my whole life through, I could never conjure up something as harmful to a human being as what I have been forced to agonize through. These things should never happen to any human being ever. Not for a day, not for a week, or a month, let alone decades as has been my plight. It is nothing short of a sickening Hitleresque experiment to see how far a person can be stretched without actually killing them. Perhaps this is what it was like to be a patient of Dr. Josef Mengele. At least the suffering his subjects were forced to endure was brief in comparison.

In our criminal justice system the act of murder is categorized according to the severity of the crime. In a case of accidental death, the defendant may be charged with manslaughter. Suddenly flying off the handle in a fit of rage is considered a lesser offense of murder, whereas carefully calculated, premeditated murder is at the top end of the spectrum. What is the crime then, when wealthy and powerful individuals implement a recipe long in existence, gaining support from government authorities along the way? It redefines the meaning of premeditation far beyond what most of us consider it to be. What I have been subject to for a quarter century is nothing less than the pre-premeditated, institutional, and systematic slaughter of a human being.

In this chapter I have shed light on just some of the adversities I have suffered. There are many more not included herein, but these are the ones that stand out most prominent in my memory. The fact I have survived to this point makes no sense at all, except that God's will will be done. He has numbered my days aright. That old devil cannot believe I am still here and I know those doing his bidding are quite confounded as well. The main point does not consist of the rotten evils that have happened to me. The things I have described in this chapter have been told to elucidate a profound reality that must be revealed: They are coming after us. Not only are they preparing to, but are and have been. They are picking up a full head of steam and are flying under the radar. They are coming at those who stand in their way. They are using any and all avenues possible. These people think they are attempting to take *over* the country, but Satan's goal is to take *down* our country. It is my declaration that Satan and those juxtaposed with him will glide along undetected no longer. Let the cloak of darkness be cast off and their endeavors be revealed to an observing world. As armed criminals being captured, their weapons of warfare must be surrendered. Among many other things, they must be disarmed from using modern technology employed invasively against American citizens. Satanic forces must be restrained. I proclaim victory is ours in Christ Jesus (1 John 5:4-5)!

Throughout all these adversities, I have called out first and foremost to my Lord, the Creator of the universe. If He heals me, then I will be healed (Jeremiah 17:14). If not, then the worst thing they can do to me is the best thing that can happen to me (Matthew 10:28). In Chapter 3 in the book of Daniel, Shadrach, Meshach, and Abednego made it known that even if God did not deliver them, there was still an imperative message that had to be understood. In no way were they going to bow down and worship any other god, but God Himself. The God these men worshipped 2,600 years ago is the same God whom I love and serve; the same God who placed a calling upon me from the time I was in my mother's womb. It is God's directive upon me and in no way do I intend to be found negligent in performing that which He is requiring of me. Contrary to what the devil and his workers of iniquity intend to accomplish, my departure from this world will not happen until my work on earth is done.

In Romans 8:28, Scripture speaks to those who love God, telling us He is using all things together for our good. That includes all of our hardships and challenges, our adversities and sufferings – He is working in all these things for our good. So, just what is His purpose in it all? What is the "good" this verse is talking about? Although there are more questions than answers when we consider this topic, I can tell you in all certainty that the "good" is inclusive of two vital factors. Firstly, in it all we are provided an opportunity to grow in our trust of Him. This trusting faith in turn provides our apprehension of and participation in the victory which has already been determined (1 John 5:4). Secondly, take a close look at the Scripture quoted at the opening of this chapter, Philippians 3:10-11. God's ultimate objective for us in this world is to get us into Heaven to be with Him. In order to achieve that, we must be resurrected from the dead. The process of participating in Christ's sufferings prepares and positions us with Christ, ultimately leading to a place wherein we may attain to the resurrection from the dead. Must all Christians suffer as a prerequisite for entry into Heaven? Fortunately not! But understand this dear friend: We are guaranteed persecution in this world (2 Timothy 3:12). God will use that opportunity (Romans 5:3-5) to shape our character and to achieve His ultimate objective (Matthew 5:10). Participating in the sufferings of Christ, although a distinct privilege, is not easy. His abiding presence provides strength to prevail. I trust this explanation helps you understand the subject in proper context. In terms of my reason for writing, there is more, much more, that needs to be understood in its proper context.

CHAPTER 11

UNDERSTANDING IT IN PROPER CONTEXT: THE BABYLONIAN SYSTEM

The woman was dressed in purple and scarlet,
and was glittering with gold, precious stones and pearls.
She held a golden cup in her hand, filled with abominable things
and the filth of her adulteries.
The name written on her forehead was a mystery:

BABYLON THE GREAT
THE MOTHER OF PROSTITUTES
AND OF THE ABOMINATIONS OF THE EARTH.

I saw that the woman was drunk with the blood
of God's holy people, the blood of those
who bore testimony to Jesus.

Revelation 17:4-6

THE CURRENT POLITICAL environment in the United States demonstrates significant division exists among the political factions. Although numerous policies of the Democratic Party track diametrically opposed to God's Word, it is important for us to understand that no person in government is exempt from running afoul regardless of party identity. Yes, there exists proliferate outright insanity among Democrats, but Republicans nor those of any other political affiliation are immune from deception. We are dealing with human beings, power, and lots of money. The heart of man is inclined toward corruption (Jeremiah 17:9). Most who enter into politics initially possess pure motives, but many become indoctrinated and corrupt; their original intents are quickly discarded as they deviate towards corruption. Our Founding Fathers recognized this and it compelled them to create a framework document, the U.S. Constitution, defining who government is and limiting the powers of those elected. They did that with ingenious foresight. Their intent was to protect our God-given freedoms, as best as possible, from those who would take advantage of positions of power, usurping control over the governed. All this being said, what we are witnessing today is demonstrative of the fact that we have come full circle, back to the circumstances which compelled both the Declaration and Constitution into existence in the first place. What we are witnessing is exactly what I quoted in chapter eight: "We pretty much have California locked up. We are going to take over the country." As a young man hearing that for the first time back in the late 1980s, I really did not lend much credence to what they were saying. It seemed so far-fetched to me and quite honestly, I was altogether oblivious to politics at that young age. Like most others at that time of life, I was impressionable; I listened to the voices around me at the workplace. Whenever I cast a ballot, my vote went for those candidates others suggested to me, to those with values leaning in a worldly direction. Years past and my inner being became more fashioned and shaped by God's indwelling presence; I became Spirit formed. The accompanying discernment granted me an ability to distinguish Godly versus worldly values. This is how God works. He does it because He loves and cares for us (Romans 12:2 and 2 Corinthians 3:16-18).

I want to pose to my readers a hypothetical situation. Let's say there was an election held wherein the leader of a country was being determined by a fair vote of the population. Now let us say that the final two candidates for that office had their credentials compared side-by-side. One was a basically a hero, having fought for that country in a time of war. He was wounded in the process to the point where it nearly cost him his life and he sustained permanent disabilities as a result. Now consider that the opposing candidate was also called upon to fight for the freedoms of that same country, for the same people casting the ballots, but he refused; he ran away the opposite direction as a young and able man when his country needed him. I think it would appear obvious to most people which candidate of these two better qualifies for leadership of that country based upon these merits alone. You are certainly free to disagree with me, but my opinion is that the latter of the two qualifies only for automatic disqualification. Allow me to reveal to you that this hypothetical situation I proposed actually happened. Not only did it happen, but the latter candidate was elected and it happened right here in the United States of America.

The presidential election of 1996 saw Bob Dole, a decorated World War II hero, lose the presidency to Bill Clinton who dodged the draft when called upon to serve his country. That was an eye-opening experience for me. It seemed obvious who the better choice was, but Americans voted for Mr. Clinton. As my analytical mind searched for reasons why, I came to the conclusion something was lacking among the people: spiritual vision. The two terms in office Clinton served in the 1990s saw an unprecedented polarization of U.S. Government bureaucracies. That polarization has taken off in a unilaterally democratic direction and all too frequently exercises an unconstitutional heavy-handedness upon American citizens. This is readily visible in government today. The division of powers contained in the three separate federal government bodies has become compromised; it is often circumvented and bypassed. There have been attempts to abolish the two-party system as well. Remember what they said, dear friend, "We pretty much have California locked up. We are going to take over the country." It is a well-known fact that many people came up dead around the Clintons and motives for murder are substantiable. Stark similarities exist throughout my experiences. Do not begin to believe foul-play occurrences are limited to a select few; there is a movement taking place. Do not even begin to think either that, just because some suddenly decided to take a nicer approach, they have stopped going after certain people. I challenge you to take notice of I have presented in this book and carefully consider how the movement has evolved. If you do not already know, I suppose you can accurately guess who the unions and California's politicians endorsed in that 1996 election.

I have sincere concerns that way too much of our populace is in that same place today: lacking spiritual vision, uninformed, and apathetic. Dear fellow American citizens, we must awaken to the ills of what is happening. We cannot and must not allow this to continue. We also need to understand that this diabolical coup is satanic in origin. An attempted complete take over is in progress and we need to stand against it. No institution of man will endure forever, including the United States of America. For the children of God, we belong to an eternal Kingdom (John 18:36). While we are still here in this world, I can say that with any measure of understanding regarding this nation's founding principles, one can comprehend that God granted us something unique and wonderful. Although our Kingdom is not of this world, in no way should we be apathetically neglectful in squandering His gift to us. Men, women, and children fleeing religious persecution made an arduous and lengthy journey across a vast ocean span in search of a place where they could enjoy the blessings of life, liberty, and the pursuit of happiness. Landing on the eastern shores of the North American Continent, they cried out to the Creator of Heaven and Earth and He granted them, and subsequently us, some of the deepest longings of humanity. Dear friend, if we fail to stand against the powers of hell that are actively attempting to destroy our country, we face the imminent threat of losing it. Not only that, but we would also be forfeiting the God-given blessings of liberty we have been the fortunate recipients of.

Throughout the history of mankind, no nation other than Israel has been as close to God as America has been. Among other things, the U.S. has been a protector of Israel. It has been said that America's Bible Belt has been Israel's safety belt. The devil has been doing everything he can to destroy Israel all along. The Bible says about the devil, "The thief comes only to steal and kill and destroy" (John 10:10). If we consider what nations around the world today other than Israel would be located within the crosshairs of that old split-hoofed fool, the devil, America tops the list. To make it unambiguously clear, the devil is attempting to destroy our beloved country, is working overtime in pursuit of that objective, and has infiltrated and deceived the Democratic Party to be his own workers of iniquity. As I said, Republicans are in no way immune to the deception. Although not exhibiting insanity to the extent of the Democratic consortium, some Republicans are also engaged participants in what amounts to nothing short of an errant rebellion against God. Resolution to our divisions will not be provided by a political party nor by mankind and the answers he proposes. The antidote for the ills of the human heart is found in Jesus Christ and in Him alone. This is not warfare being something in the way of Democrat versus Republican. Neither is the battle being waged against flesh and blood. This is good versus evil. This is God and His own standing against the devil's schemes (Ephesians 6:10-18). What we are witnessing in the United States of America today is nothing short of the emergence of a satanic world system; this is a Babylonian insurgency.

Listed in Scripture more than 280 times, Babylon is second only to Jerusalem as the most often mentioned of cities. Every single time the context is negative. An opportunistic pathogen, she represents a religious and immoral prostitute who merges with and manipulates government powers. Babylon is symbolically representative of sinful humanity and is an apostate culture in rebellion against God. She possesses a profound propensity for self-delusion, selfish ambition, and sinful pride. She is demonically depraved and persecutes God's people. The ultimate fate has already been determined: Babylon will inevitably will be destroyed (Revelation 18:8).

The first use of the title Babylon can be traced all the way back to Genesis 10:10, to a man named Nimrod who was the grandson of Ham who was himself the son of Noah. Some Biblical scholars believe the name Nimrod means "we will revolt." He was the rebel founder of a few cities, one of the most well-known being Babel in the area between the Tigris and Euphrates Rivers. This is where his descendants constructed the infamous Tower of Babel noted in Genesis Chapter 11. Another one of those cities was the actual city of Babylon. Among the descendants of Nimrod were the Assyrians and the Babylonians who were notoriously ruthless conquerors that vexed and vanquished their neighbors throughout the ancient world, inclusive of the Israelites. Perhaps the world's earliest dictator, Nimrod was the first great Gentile world power to persecute God's people, a mighty leader in rebellion against the Lord.

In the Old Testament, the city of Babylon was the capitol of the ancient Babylonian Empire. Its history spanned some two millennia, from about 2300 BC to 325 BC. Babylonian myth claimed it was built by the chief god of Babylon, Marduk, and stood just South of modern-day Baghdad, Iraq. This was the powerful empire that conquered the Assyrians, Judah, and Israel between 605 BC and 582 BC under the leadership of King Nebuchadnezzar. The Old Testament book of Daniel provides background and insight into the workings of the Babylonian Empire. Babylon epitomized sin and defiance against God, being a center of idolatry, occult, and immorality.

References to Babylon in the New Testament are frequently made, but in a completely different context; not in specific reference to the ancient empire and its capitol city. During the Apostolic Age, the use of the title was synonymous with Rome. In the book of Revelation, Babylon appears again in the last days. Throughout history, well-meaning individuals and even Biblical scholars have attempted to identify Babylon geographically, applying the label to a variety of specific nations. Claims today range from Rome, to the Papacy, to ancient Babylon resurrected. It has even been postulated that Russia, Iran, or the United States may be *the* Babylon. Considering there are such a wide variety of perspectives on the subject, which one is correct? I submit to you for your consideration that, although Babylon may eventually become prominent as a specific designated geographic locale, it has been and will be present in a variety of places. Allow me to explain.

From Nimrod to Nebuchadnezzar to Rome, Babylon operates in rebellion against God, meanwhile an underlying theme revealing her true identity begins to emerge. Babylon epitomizes a world system, satanic in origin, arises from within a society, commandeers power, and persecutes God's people. That is the veritable nature of what Babylon symbolizes. As I mentioned, often times when reading through the book of Revelation people attempt to identify a specific nation in the world today that is Babylon. What history has evidenced is that several nations have met this definition; several nations have experienced the rise of a diabolical sysytem from within. In every instance the government was infilitrated and subsequently succumbed. Freedoms were usurped and God-fearing people persecuted while the diabolical system established absolute control and authority. This is the exact mindset that led our ancient foe, the devil, to be expelled from Heaven. Couple that with man's greed, his hunger for power, and an insatiable quest to fulfill fleshly desires and the result is recipe for disaster. All these things embody precisely what Babylon is as described in Revelation.

Looking beyond the speculation and possibilities of what country or city she is, Scripture makes it distinctly clear Babylon will possess great religious and political significance in the last days. We can accurately understand from Revelation 17 that she represents a religious and moral prostitute who merges with and manipulates government powers. To apprehend a proper understanding is to recognize that

Babylon is not merely a specific geographically defined nation or city, but rather a satanic world system. That nefarious system rises up from within preexistent government systems attempting to usurp complete control and establish uncontested dominance. Babylon is a diabolical system rather than an established government. This was true of ancient Babylon, Empirical Rome, Nazi Germany, a number of other world governments, and will again rear its ugly head in the days to come as we approach the imminent return of Jesus Christ. She persecutes God's people with increasing measure (Revelation 17:6). The good news is that she will ultimately and inevitably be destroyed (Revelation 14:8; 16:19; 18:2, 10, 21), much to the jubilation of the redeemed children of God (Revelation 19:1-3).

With some measure of spiritual discernment, one may recognize the emergence of the Babylonian system in the world today. If your own eyes lay hold of something described within the pages of Scripture, you can take that to the bank. When one witnesses a system rise up within a government – an apostate, self-seeking, prideful, and sin promoting system – then one can know whenceforth it cometh. If and when we witness a system arise that attempts to usurp complete control, displacing long-established Christian-Judeo values and persecutes those identified as bearing testimony to Jesus, then we should be mindful of the things Scripture reveals to us.

Does anything here seem familiar to you in any way? Does anything in the world around you today appear eerily reminiscent of this subject we are addressing? Well it should, especially if you are a child of God. Make no mistake, loved ones, the Babylonian system is alive and operating in the world even now.

Throughout history Satan has attempted to wipe out God's people. That ancient foe attempted it at the very beginning in the Garden of Eden. He tried it again with the Egyptian Pharaoh, the Moabites, the Canaanites, the Assyrians, and the Babylonians. Antiochus Epiphanes and the Greco-Syrian forces came against Israel. The Roman army destroyed Jerusalem not once, but twice. The Jewish people have been scattered and persecuted throughout the world for the past two thousand years. More recently, when a Babylonian system of government rose to power in Nazi Germany, Adolph Hitler oversaw the extermination of over six million Jews, nearly equal to the entire number residing in Israel today. Immediately following World War II, Egypt, Jordan, and Syria promptly attacked Israel. Even today they are under constant threat from Palestinians and jihadists. Iran's own president and commanding generals have vowed to "wipe Israel off the map." We cannot afford to mistakenly believe all this comes from peoples, nations, and religions which have harbored animosity toward God's chosen people. These repeated attempts specifically targeting Israel have been initiated by no other than Satan himself. Consider this if you would: Why has this been an unending, perpetual agenda, unceasing throughout human history? Furthermore, how could this small, overmatched group of people possibly have survived all this were God not orchestrating the very events which have seen them through thus far? Simply put, it is otherwise impossible; they would not have survived.

The truth is, Israel's enemies have been numerous and formidable, but they are no match for our sovereign God, God who in fact "presides over the destinies of nations," as Patrick Henry so accurately pointed out. Such has been the circumstance for the United States of America as well. Persecuted and oppressed people came from distant lands seeking a place to freely worship their Creator. They petitioned Him and He granted them their requests. We as Americans today have inherited and enjoy the benefits of what God ordained in granting people called by His Name, Christian people, a place to freely embrace Him. We now enjoy governmental protections of the rights He endowed us with, at least for the time being. The U.S. has a special place in the heart of God. No, we are not His chosen people as is Israel. Just like Israel, however, we can in retrospective analysis observe God's sovereign hand has been upon us all along. We were no match for the British during the war for independence. Entering World War II, we had the thirteenth or fourteenth largest army in the world, yet emerged from those atrocities the world's preeminent superpower. There have been so many things that could have been our undoing, but God who, "presides over the destinies of nations," has presided over this nation. This is especially true of those who have humbled themselves before Him; for those nations who have prayed and turned from wickedness, seeking His face (2 Chronicles 7:14) as has been the legacy of the United States of America.

What is more is that the U.S. as a nation has become a contemporary and vital constituent of the Abrahamic Covenant found in Genesis 12:3. God tells Abraham in that verse of Scripture that He will bless those who bless them (Abraham/Israel) while cursing those who curse them. This promise has proven true throughout history. The former component of the Covenant outlines criteria in which God's provision of blessing may be received. America has been a tremendous blessing and protector of Israel and God has blessed us for that. As I previously stated, America's Bible Belt has been Israel's safety belt. Let us never lose that! I do not know about you, but if God tells me that I can be blessed by Him in some way, then by all means I want that! How about you? The latter component of the Abrahamic Covenant has also proven true time and time again. Nation after nation has persecuted Israel only to experience their own demise. Scripture refers to Israel as the apple of God's eye (Deuteronomy 32:10 and Zechariah 2:8). Casper ten Boom, father of Corrie ten Boom, said about Nazi Germany, "I pity them, Corrie. They have touched the apple of God's eye." Let me offer some wise advice to any of those who may be contemplating otherwise: Do not mess with the apple of God's eye. This is no fairytale based upon religious mysticism. This is the Living Word of the One, True, and real Living God.

Up to this point in this chapter I have attempted to illustrate a point I wish to make and it is my intention to convey an accurate understanding. It is my hope that I was able to demonstrate to you, the reader, the current circumstances we face in the world today. Perhaps it is something you have already become aware of, at least maybe in part. Many Christians see the events transpiring today, the world unravelling before us, and they look up and say, "My redemption draws near" (Luke 21:28). We are seeing things occur today that we never imagined we would witness in our lifetimes. Scripture warns us regarding these events; we knew they were coming. For so many of us, we just did not think that we would be here during these times. Somehow, they just seemed far off somewhere in the distant future beyond our lifetimes. We are astounded at the cultural moral filth and decay eroding our own society right here in the United States. It is incumbent upon me to come right out and state what is observable to the spiritually discerning: A Babylonian insurgency is taking place in the United States of America today. I am not saying that America *is* Babylon. Although that could possibly be what eventually evolves from this depravation, I really do not think America is Babylon. I pray we are not and certainly many others do as well. As a nation, we occupy a special place in the heart of our Creator and can be assured He is not done with us yet.

We may be wondering why God allows things to continue as they are and seems to just sit idly by. 2 Peter 3:9 tells us, "The Lord is not slow in keeping his promise, as some understand slowness. Instead he is patient with you, not wanting anyone to perish, but everyone to come to repentance." His ultimate objective for humanity in this world is the salvation of our souls. Our Creator stays His hand of judgment because He has a plan to set men free – free from the curse of sin and death. He is calling people out of darkness into His light. He beckons His creation to make peace with Him. The question is: Do you hear Him? Have you made peace God, dear friend? If not, now is the time. Do not put it off any longer.

The child of God has been issued a directive to keep the fire within burning (Matthew 25:1-13). Enduring to the end and participating in the harvest, we must achieve and maintain a cohesive unity in the Body of Christ (1 Corinthians 12:25). Mankind has erected many barriers within the Church. We can be so focused on doctrinal differences that we divide ourselves. Denominational barriers must not serve so as to prevent unity. We need to be fully aware that our divisiveness has the capacity to impact in such a way that can cause people to abandon the faith altogether. I really do not want to have to answer to God for that. I suspect that you feel the same way also. Abraham Lincoln has been quoted as saying, "A house divided against itself cannot stand." When President Lincoln gave those words in a speech, they were not his own, but rather a direct quote from Scripture (Mark 3:25). Dear saints of the Living God, we must stand together. If we do not, then we will fall and potentially cause others to also in the process. Making every effort to avoid division, we must possess cohesive unity in the Church. We must achieve and maintain homeostasis in the Body of Christ.

CHAPTER 12

HOMEOSTASIS IN THE BODY

Continue to remember those in prison as if you
were together with them in prison, and those
who are mistreated as if you yourselves were suffering.

Hebrews 13:3

As it is, there are many parts, but one body.

1 Corinthians 12:20

If one part suffers, every part suffers with it;
if one part is honored, every part rejoices with it.

1 Corinthians 12:26

CONSIDERING MY NUMEROUS encounters with uranium, it only stands to reason that I would become informed about the substance. Forgoing a career in toxicology, I have autodidactically gleaned knowledge in specific regards to certain toxins and how they impact our bodies. To clarify, it is important to be aware that a number of other poisons are being used, but it turns out this radioactive element is the perfect poison. In the case of exposure to a nuclear accident or detonated weaponry, potassium iodide can be orally ingested to protect the thyroid gland from radiation injury. These safeguard measures are only effective for about the first 24 hours as uranium is rapidly dispersed into bodily tissues. Our bodies identify it as calcium and utilize it as such: for muscle contraction, heart rhythm, and building bone and teeth. It binds tenaciously wherever it is deposited and there are no known ameliorating agents established to be effective. Since uranium transfers quickly from blood to tissues, conventional blood and urine analysis are not reliable indicators for its presence after the first day. Hair analysis for toxic elements, therefore, may be the most dependable means to determine its existence in the human body and that requiring several days post exposure. If a person is a victim of uranium poisoning and the toxin is administered in small quantities involving several doses over a period of time, then one may begin to understand how uranium is in fact a perfect poison. By the time one realizes something may have happened to them, well more than 24 hours have elapsed. All the while it remains in the body it continues to be radioactive, carcinogenic, and grossly disruptive to homeostasis.

Homeostasis is a term used in reference to the constant dynamics of an internal environment achieving a condition of optimal functioning. Internal systems, biological and chemical, all working together in proper equilibrium facilitate life and health. With resistance to external adverse factors, biological organisms can begin to thrive. This is the status of a healthy human body. I have borrowed this term from the fields of biology and applied it to the Body of Christ. Reading through the latter twenty verses of 1 Corinthians 12, we can visualize a variety of core components inextricably linked that must function in concert. If and when those components become antagonistic to each another, the entire system experiences breakdown. This is true for the human body and it is true for the Body of Christ. We have become focused on things that make us different. How can we exhibit resistance to change when change it-self becomes a dividing factor? How could we possibly demonstrate to the world our status as His disciples like we are supposed to ac-cording to John 13:35? In that capacity, how can the Body of Christ even begin to exercise any resistance against external adversities? How in God's creation are we going to withstand an onslaught from the devil when he occupies positions of influence, wealth, and power?! It is imperative in these last days that we attain and main-tain cohesive unity. It is essential for the constituents to function collectively to achieve and sustain homeostasis in the Church as a whole, in the Body of Christ.

Proper identification of an enemy is crucial to effective and suc-cessful combat. Familiarity with armament and weaponry is neces-sary. Utilization of these resources will prove futile if one rides off into battle as the Lone Ranger. We need to know what we are up against, train with and employ the armor issued to us, and proceed against the enemy in joint military force. The enemy is not com-prised of persons, but rather is the devil and his schemes (Ephesians 6:11-12). Certainly people do the devil's work; it is happening all around us. We are challenged to be mindful that Christ died for them too and longs for that same personal relationship we delight in and benefit from. It is okay to hate what they do, but as difficult as it may be, we must view them as Jesus does: with love. This is actually a part of the warfare we are engaged in. It is with the Word of God we defeat our inclinations to conduct ourselves in contrary manner. With it we also learn to love our enemies. The Word of God is powerful, dividing correctly, unlike our human propensities. The Word of God is our solitary instrument of offense; it is Sword of the Spirit (Ephesians 6:17).

Military forces of the United States and their equipment are de-scribed as G.I., or Government Issue. As enlisted service members in God's Army, Christians are issued five pieces of defensively protective equipment (Ephesians 6:13-17). Any defense afforded by mankind is wholly insufficient to effectively equip military personnel engaged in spiritual warfare. Knowing what we have need of before we ask, God allocates to us G.I., or God Issued armor. Dear friend, there is a war going on and if you are a child of God, then make no mistake, you are a G.I. yourself.

Accurate identification of the enemy, possession and proper utilization of adequate equipment, and remaining in connection with God and His family all work in harmony to bring about spiritual homeostasis in us individually. Members of the Body of Christ occupying their designated anatomical positions facilitate the physiology of a united body, the Body of Christ. Equilibrium balances, vital signs are within normal range, and the resulting status is homeostasis.

In America, Christians have been relatively exempt from the oppression and persecution faced elsewhere in the world today and throughout history. This fact is both a component of and evidence of God's blessing upon the U.S.A. We cannot take it for granted, however. Not only have we erected unnecessary divisions in the Church, but prevailing apathy has held us in its grasp and we are lacking spiritual vision. Around us we have witnessed the moral degradation of our society accompanied with appalling government policies and procedures in direct defiance of God. I consider the absurd hypothesis mankind evolved from an ape and contemplate that perhaps the opposite holds true: Man did not evolve *from* an ape, but appears at times to be *devolving into* one. It is time for a spiritual awakening in our country, loved ones. The time is right and the time is now. In it all a harvest of human souls can and will take place, rescuing many from the eternal torment of Hell.

My brothers and sisters in Christ, as we engage the battle, let us proceed dressed in the full armor of God. Let us move into battle together, inextricably linked with God and with one another. Being apathetic cannot and will not result in our victory. It is imperative that we procure and preserve open lines of communication, in no way facilitating adversarial falsehoods – the lies of commission and omission which will sever our bonds. Although the final outcome has already been secured, we have a fight on our hands. The Babylonian system rearing its ugly head in America must be put to flight. The devil must be defeated. We need to prayerfully and assertively make a pronouncement, declaring over this nation: We are His people; we are a Christian nation! With Heavenly Armor, let us enter in to the holy place of God's promises.

CONCLUSION: GOD'S WILL *WILL* BE DONE!

Why do the nations conspire and the peoples plot in vain?
The kings of the earth rise up and the rulers band together
against the LORD and against his anointed, saying, "Let us
break their chains and throw off their shackles." The One
enthroned in heaven laughs; the Lord scoffs at them. He
rebukes them in his anger and terrifies them in his wrath,
saying, "I have installed my king on Zion, my holy mountain." I will proclaim the LORD's decree: He said to me,
"You are my son; today I have become your father. Ask
me, and I will make the nations your inheritance, the ends
of the earth your possession. You will break them with
a rod of iron; you will dash them to pieces like pottery."
Therefore, you kings, be wise; be warned, you rulers of the
earth. Serve the LORD with fear and celebrate his rule with
trembling. Kiss his son, or he will be angry and your way
will lead to your destruction, for his wrath can flare up in a
moment. Blessed are all who take refuge in him.

Psalm 2

IT IS MY sincere hope and prayer that, having read this book, many people will become aware of the things I have shared herein. Undoubtedly, many people will read this book and hopefully, it even makes it into the hands of some in government. There will be those who will lash out at me, some of whom have been doing so for a long time anyway. They will do everything they can to label me a crazy person and will attempt to convince others also. This is nothing new to me. They have not only been slandering me for years on end, they have sought to outright slaughter me. It is no wonder the Holy Spirit impressed upon me this ministry verse: "Rescue those being led away to death; hold back those staggering toward slaughter" (Proverbs 24:11). Go ahead, label me whatever you want to, I do not care. I have been marked by my Creator a peculiar display to the ways of mankind and the world. I know where I stand with my Lord; I have made peace with Him. Have you?

There exists an imperative that every person must understand. Please allow me to make this point unambiguously clear: Under no circumstance, never ever make an agreed upon settlement without informing all parties involved, including the targeted person or persons. There may be certain extenuating circumstances under your consideration warranting an undisclosed settlement. Please understand, with these people and their satanic agenda, you would only be serving so as to pave the way for an execution of evil beyond what you ever could have imagined. Do not do it!

In the Gospel of John Chapter 9, Jesus healed a blind man. As it turned out, the event was not so much about that man's physiological ability to see, but rather about certain leaders and their *in*ability to see *spiritually*. Jesus healed the man born blind to illustrate the spiritual blindness of certain leaders. In America we have been blessed with the ability to choose our leaders. When that process takes place, my observation is that most of us make choices based upon the personalities of the candidates – people we like that appeal to us. Charming individuals gifted with refined and eloquent speaking abilities more often than not garner public interest. They possess the gift of the gab.

They just say the right things that itching ears long to hear (2 Timothy 4:3-4). When the imminent appearance of the Antichrist finally manifests, which is rapidly approaching, he will be an eloquent orator himself (Revelation 13:5), employing that ability to sway masses in the process of executing widespread deception (Daniel 7:25). We must therefore ask ourselves, 'Are we being deceived?' If so, how do we know if we are? If we are deceived, then we really do not know it because we are in fact, deceived.

The fact of the matter is that politicians in the United States have become quite fine-tuned in marketing their wares, aiming to sell us on who they are and what they are offering. Consider the marketing strategies of supermarkets and television commercials. They come at us in ways we are completely unaware of. From candy placed at a child's eye level in the slow-moving checkout lane, to the music playing in the background, to even the mood-altering color schemes of the environment, subliminal strategies are constantly being utilized unbeknownst to us. Using the proper lure and bait, a fisherman hooks a prized fish. Such are the tactics found within the tackleboxes belonging to contemporary American politicians and leaders elsewhere alike. Propaganda techniques are intensely studied, well-rehearsed, and launched upon oblivious humanity. It almost seems unfair, but it is a harsh reality – the truth. Their hope is that they will be able to retain us in some kind of catatonic state, much like a mushroom: placing us in the dark and fertilizing us with defecated waste products from an uncastrated male bovine. Please excuse my euphemistic utilization of vocabulary, though it is indeed fitting. We may not realize when we are being deceived, but we can and must awaken from it, see the truth for what it is, and be set free from spiritual blindness.

When choosing the people we elect to office, we need to refocus our attention away from persons and their personalities and instead zero-in on the issues before us. There will be those whom we may perceive as abrasive in some way. Others we may find appealing in their charm and wittiness, possessing eloquent speaking abilities. We cannot be focused on these criteria as determining factors when approaching the ballot box. These character attributes and liabilities possess an overwhelming propensity to deceive. We must look beyond the individual and emphasize the issues: Where does the candidate stand on protecting my God-given freedoms particularly as outlined in our founding documents? Will they swear to uphold the Constitution, then actually do so? Do they produce some kind of interpretation of the Constitution or accurately apply its words in direct quotation? Where do they stand in regards to freedom of speech or freedom of religion? How about taking, or rather not taking, so much of our personal possessions or hard-earned income? Do they believe parents have the right to determine what their children learn in schools or the choice of what school they attend? What is their position on the Second Amendment? The sanctity of human life? What about the strength of our military? A free market economy? Time-tested and proven traditional values? There are a multitude of issues. Each is of paramount importance and relevant to every single one of us. Political candidates stand diametrically opposed to one another in regards to where they stand on these issues, yet put forth valiant efforts to distort any distinction. We need to focus on the issues we face with a particular emphasis on our freedoms and the protections thereof. We must not determine we will vote for an individual by default swayed by colleagues and collectivism or simply because we like them or are loyal to their political party, all the while rejecting another because we do not care for their personality. A careful assessment may reveal the latter's values to actually be more reflective of ours. Better yet, that candidate might just be a person God raised up for such a time as this. It makes perfect sense that if God has ordained an individual to take up office in American politics, a certain kind boldness will be a personality trait required when it comes to standing against the evils we war against today. If we continue to simply look for the individuals who appear most appealing to us, those whose personalities we like best, then we leave ourselves vulnerable to deception and become like the prize fish caught by a cleverly devised political marketing scheme disguised as a mesmerizing lure. I think the American people are far too intelligent to continue to be held in the deception of spiritual blindness. We can and must embark upon a spiritual awakening across this great nation of ours or we risk losing it.

In America we possess a tendency to associate quality leadership with an ability to effectively exercise dominance over others. Individuals pursue careers in positions of leadership often because they are simply going after their own interests and want control over people. What are held in high esteem as quality leadership traits actually pose risk of harm. That entire concept of ideal leadership needs to be completely inverted. In the Gospel of Mark 10:41-45, Jesus presents an accurate model of quality leadership. He describes a person devoid of arrogance and self-exaltation. The truth be told, humility and serving others as outlined in that passage of Scripture are attributes to not only be strongly required of leaders, but they need to be inherent characteristics. We will not identify any human being who is perfect in this regard, but they must at the very least be moving in that direction. This is true not only in the context of a Biblical model, but it was the original intent of American government. Our elected individuals were supposed to be serving the people and the government was supposed to be We the People. They are supposed to be serving us. Something has changed. Possessing these character attributes and conducting oneself in proper utilization of them is not only demonstrative quality leadership, but reveals a person's heart intent. It reveals that they are not pursuing and occupying political office motivated by selfish ambition nor by diabolical influence. For so many years my prayer has been that God would cast His light into the concealing darkness throughout our government. I pray He reveals truth, allowing the people of this nation to accurately see it for what it is, sans deception. I pray that He would prevent wayward individuals from obtaining political positions. I pray He removes those currently occupying office who conduct themselves in a manner contrary His will. My diligent prayer has been and continues to be that we, We the People, would avail ourselves accordingly at the ballot box as we move to secure the blessings of liberty to ourselves and our posterity. My sincere hope and prayer is that you do likewise.

As I finish, allow me to submit to you the following questions: If there exists even the slightest possibility that anything I have told you is true, then should not there be a cause for serious concern? Should not there be a response that recognizes the events and experiences I have endured as inherently evil? Recall that quote from the introduction, "Truth sounds like hate to those that hate the truth." Let the facts be candid to the discerning: Truth offends those who do not want to hear it. If what I have written here offends someone, then does that not reveal where they stand? If standing against evil is undesirable, then what is really going on in that person's heart? If what I am saying elicits lashing out and rage, then that reveals what is truly in their hearts. Such a person is unmistakably revealing that they too have the same desperate and most common need all human beings possess: the need for Jesus Christ; the need for Him and the peace that only He, the Prince of Peace can bring. Dear friend, do not be deceived, but be aware. The conflict raging around us is a battle between good and evil. Satan and his minions erect mazes with smoke and mirrors in performing their circus acts. All the while they attempt to convince that the battle lines are drawn in places such as race, gender, what schools are teaching children, political parties, and even religion. If we become ensnared by buying into these falsehoods, then wedges of division are driven into these very places. Do not become trapped by that! Do not be deceived! This battle is a battle between good and evil; this is the reality of where the battle lines truly exist. The ultimate prize in it all is the human soul. Dearly loved by God, ask Him to grant you spiritual visual acuity to see through Satan's magic acts of deception and to accurately see truth for what it is. That has been and continues to be my prayer, both for myself and for all the inhabitants of this land. May the Creator of all things grant us proper knowledge of *the* Truth (John 14:6)!

As children of God, we ultimately belong to an eternal Kingdom that is not of this world. Meanwhile, we cannot be neglectful in regards to what has been entrusted to our care. I love the United States of America; I am an American patriot through and through. I dearly love our country and possess a strong desire to see it embrace the One who granted us this nation in the first place. This country is something unique and special among all the nations of the earth. If our citizenry surrenders their hearts to Jesus in any measure, it will inevitably result in greatly need change throughout this land of the free and the home of the brave. Jesus Christ transforms human beings from the inside out. Changed people leads to changed families, which in turn leads to changed communities, and to changed cities. It can and will lead to entire societies changed for the better. May we fully herein realize that distinct change found nowhere else but in Jesus Christ and embark upon a new and better direction in our United States of America; in your United States of America, oh Lord!

It is one thing to believe in Jesus, but it is a whole other thing to give Him your heart. The Bible tells us that even demons believe in God (James 2:19). He desires so much more from us than just that. Let me ask, do you know that feeling you have when you love a person? That feeling when you care about them so much that you would do anything for them? That is something present only in relationships where we know and love each other. That is precisely what our Creator longs to have with us. He feels that way about you. Do you feel the same about Him? God loves you so much that He would do anything for you, including laying down His own life, which is exactly what He did in seeking that kind of relationship with you. Perfection had to be sacrificed to pave the way for the imperfect. Jesus is that perfection; He paid the ultimate sacrifice. You and I are imperfect, but the way has been paved for us to approach His Throne of Grace and enter in a deep abiding relationship with the One who created us.

Jesus did not stop there when He died on that cross for you and me. He was buried in a grave, but that grave could not hold Him; He came out of it. Jesus conquered the grave for all who will put their trust in him. The Resurrection of Jesus Christ is the lynchpin of the Christian faith; everything hinges upon it. If all Jesus did was die for our sins, then our sins are forgiven and that is that. But He wants more; He wants that personal relationship with us. Jesus Christ rose from the grave so that we can do likewise and go to be with Him forever. Do you believe that, my friend? The Bible says, "If you declare with your mouth, 'Jesus is Lord,' and believe in your heart that God raised him from the dead, you will be saved" (Romans 10:9). I want to invite you to enter into that relationship with Him right now. If that is your sincere desire, then speak to God the prayer on the following page. Make it your prayer to Him.

Dear Heavenly Father, I want a loving relationship with you. I am sorry for all the sin in my life. I believe Jesus died on the cross for my sins. I receive your forgiveness through the shed blood of Christ. I believe Jesus rose from the dead. As I follow You, I will do the same. I ask you to now fill me with you Holy Spirit. Here is my heart Lord, I give it to you. Wash me, cleanse me, mold me, make me, use me, and guide me. May I live with you Lord forever, Jesus my Lord. In Jesus name I pray, Amen.

"Look, I am coming soon! My reward is with me, and I will give to each person according to what they have done. I am the Alpha and the Omega, the First and the Last, the Beginning and the End."

Revelation 22:12-13

Maranatha!
Even so, come quickly, Lord Jesus!

www.ingramcontent.com/pod-product-compliance
Lightning Source LLC
Chambersburg PA
CBHW03235280326
41935CB00008B/539